Praise for *Every Student Deserves a Gifted Education*

"Brian applied a growth mindset as a teacher and principal and now applies it in his book. Our educational system does not provide gifted education for every child—**yet**. Reflections from educators and influential books, podcasts, and interviews illustrate the value of Brian's 5-shift path to create the schools we all want for our children. The principles and team culture he describes for Pre-K-12 educators apply equally to teaching recent medical school graduates to become physicians and surgeons. This is a valuable read for anyone who wants to be a better educator. Let's get all our children into the 'smart class.'"

—Steven L. Frick, MD, Professor and Vice Chair, Education, Stanford University School of Medicine, Department of Orthopaedic Surgery

"I have always been a fierce proponent of providing 'soft floors and high ceilings' for all students. However, this book removes the ceiling altogether. Before reading his book, I was an advocate for widening the gifted program net and providing access to more students. Butler rocked my world with his eloquent and impassioned case for providing access to gifted education to all students. He challenges us to move from gifted programs for some to embedded gifted programming for all."

—Ken Williams, Speaker and Author of *Ruthless Equity*

"The title of this book sums up Brian's mission with simplicity: Every student *deserves* a gifted education. How can we educators continue to label select students in early childhood as gifted and talented and complacently imply that all the rest of the students are ungifted and nontalented? Brian gently helps us work through this cognitive dissonance and rethink the status quo with stories and examples that help the reader envision what school should be. His anecdotes inspire and clarify how we can embrace a few shifts in our practices to help us move from traditional gifted education for a select few to make it the floor for all. After working with Brian at two different schools for over a dozen years, I know he is a master capacity builder. Now that talent shines through the written word, chapter by chapter, as he builds our capacity to rethink gifted education."

—Jacquie Heller, Educational Consultant and
Author of *Literacy in a PLC at Work*

"Brian (and his entire team) did what sounded impossible to this parent: they challenged each child in each aspect of all subjects no matter the test results for each child. If a normally high-performing child had an issue with a topic, perhaps multiplying fractions, the instruction was changed to match that. When a child was ahead, the instruction sped up to continue to challenge them. Each child received a concierge-level education specifically tailored in real-time to meet their needs and abilities. I would not have believed it had I not seen it. Brian knows exactly what he is doing."

—Rock Rockenbach, Former Parent Teacher Organization President,
Mason Crest Elementary School, Attorney,
Retired Military Officer

"This highly engaging book presents a powerful argument for an education system that truly believes in the unlimited potential of every child in its care. Brian Butler shares powerful strategies for manifesting a vision of rich and engaging learning. In each chapter, you will find a beautiful balance of practical ideas, compelling research, and a narrative heart. For those educators and leaders who are exploring the idea of reimagining education, this book is an important and compelling read."

—Katie White, Author of *Softening the Edges*
and Educational Consultant

"In *Every Student Deserves a Gifted Education*, Brian Butler challenges us to step off a well-worn yet ineffective and inequitable path of gifted education for the few and instead forge a new path through an educational landscape in which the gifts of all students are embraced and nourished. The combination of compelling stories and encouraging anecdotes with practical examples of practice provides guideposts for the new path.

"As a principal and assistant superintendent, I often found myself embroiled in conflicts about gifted and talented programs' exclusion and favoritism rather than student success. The children of the most vocal parents benefited from additional resources and enriched opportunities, while the majority of students received fewer opportunities because precious resources were diverted to those 3 to 5% fortunate enough to receive the 'gifted' label. In *Every Student Deserves a Gifted Education*, Brian Butler describes a different culture in which the gifts of all students are embraced and nourished. I could have used this book with my teacher teams as we designed systems to ensure an enriched education for all students, and I could have used this book to help me in those often-heated meetings!"

—Jeffrey Craig, Ed.D., retired Assistant Superintendent, Principal-Coach, and Adjunct Professor at the State University of New York College at Cortland and State University of New York at Oswego

"Brian Butler has written a most relevant and powerful book for educators. He has done the work at the highest level, and this work is filled with inspirational insights and tools for those who seek to make a real difference for all students. This is a most worthwhile read, and I am already quoting sections to the leaders and students in my district."

—Jack Baldermann, Superintendent, CUSD 201, Westmont, Illinois

"In a sea of educational literature, *Every Student Deserves a Gifted Education* shines like a beacon, offering a transformative journey through the realm of education. Brian Butler's work doesn't merely present ideas; it presents a roadmap for revolutionizing the educational landscape. The need for a paradigm shift in education has long been acknowledged, but this book addresses this need with an urgency that resonates. Butler's research is nothing short of a guiding light, grounding his assertions in a solid foundation of evidence and personal experience. This book doesn't just hint at change; it demands it.

"What truly sets this book apart is its ability to make this shift accessible, doable, personal, and logical. It's a celebration of individuality, a tribute to passion, and an ode to the potential within each and every student. Brian Butler's work is a manifesto of hope, a rallying cry for change, and a reminder that the power to nurture greatness lies within our collective hands."

—Gavin Grift, Author of *Mastering Meetings That Matter*,
Consultant, President, Grift Education,
Melbourne, Australia

"As a parent of children with a wide scope of needs, I want their teachers to have Brian's book. It clearly lays out the 'why' and follows it up with the 'how.' Teachers will leave understanding that once we know the needs of our students, we know how to meet them."

—Geri Parscale, Educational Consultant,
Author and Speaker

"Brian's passion is clearly felt in this must-read book for all educators and parents with young children. There are many gaps in our current educational system regarding providing a quality and gifted education for all students. Brian has proven what can be accomplished with true team teaching and a growth mindset. Through his experience as a student-athlete and years as a school principal, Brian has created a vision and a 5-shift path that can be used to create what we would all want for our children: a gifted education. This book will inspire and guide those who have the courage to challenge the status quo. As Brian describes, let's change the 'I can't' to 'I can't yet' and seek to bring out the very best gifts that EACH child has to offer."

—Kenny Barer, Associate Director of Mohawk Day Camp, Former Head College Basketball Coach, Former Professional Basketball Player, and Father of 3 Adult Children

"An impactful read on a topic that is historically overlooked in traditional education. Brian sheds light on current trends in public education and Gifted and Talented programs, which are stuck in a time warp. Educators desperately need to read, absorb, and implement the research-based practices outlined in this book."

—Robyn Dawson, ERZ Director, Arkansas

"This book changed my approach to teaching and interacting with students. The section in Chapter Four about harvesting student strengths was especially powerful for me. It provided a new perspective on identifying, capturing, and empowering the strengths of all students, not just those traditionally labeled as 'good students.' As a teacher who thought I was already good at this skill, Brian's book expanded the horizon for which I can capitalize on my students' strengths!"

—Jaivon Smallwood, Physical Education Teacher

"Attention, all educators, parents, and advocates of education who genuinely want to empower students! Prepare to be captivated by *Every Student Deserves a Gifted Education*. Brian Butler is an expert who provides school leaders with this transformative guide, which serves as a rallying cry for a new learning era that cherishes individuality and untapped potential. As I immersed myself in its pages, the book's emphasis on personalization struck me like a lightning bolt. No more cookie-cutter 'one-size-fits-all-all' education; it's about acknowledging the 'extraordinary' in every student. The stories of students discovering and flourishing in their passions were nothing short of inspirational, reigniting my belief in the power of personalized learning.

"In my journey through these pages, I rediscovered my passion for teaching and learning and nurturing students' individual gifts and attributes. Brian understands the importance of amplifying strengths rather than dwelling on weaknesses and gives teachers a blueprint of how to do this for themselves. Witnessing Brian's passionate call for a pedagogical shift left me empowered and ready to embark on a mission to nurture students' talents. *Every Student Deserves a Gifted Education* is a powerful reminder that education should be a vehicle for self-discovery, growth, and empowerment. This book is a must-read for anyone who envisions a world where every student's brilliance is kindled."

—Dr. Don Parker, Author of *Building Bridges*
and *Be the Driving Force*

Every Student Deserves a Gifted Education

Every Student Deserves a Gifted Education

5 Shifts to Nurturing Each Student's Unique Strengths, Passions, and Talents

Brian Butler

Published by

THE ANSWER'S
IN THE ROOM
P R E S S

To contact the author about speaking, workshops, or bulk orders of this book, visit https://www.brianbutler.info

ISBN (paperback): 979-8-9888579-0-7
ISBN (ebook): 979-8-9888579-1-4

Editor: David Aretha
Book design: Christy Day, Constellation Book Services

Library of Congress Control Number: 2023916468

Printed in the United States of America

Contents

Learning Experiences

References and Resources

Important to Note: Using This Book

Whenever you see **"Here's a Story"** in this book, a fictional story follows it. These stories are crafted to give readers unique insights and practical illustrations. The characters and events within the stories are fictional. However, I use the real names of people who have influenced me throughout my personal and professional life to celebrate them. Using these stories, I aim to help readers remember and apply the ideas presented in each section, offering them a window into how these issues manifest in their educational settings.

Throughout the book, you will also notice **"Thought Spark Questions"** for educators to reflect on and assess their current reality concerning the previously read section.

In some sections, there is open space after the questions designed for the reader to write directly in the book. This allows the reader to make notes or answer questions, deepening the reflections and giving a chance to pause before moving on to the next section.

Foreword

My life changed in 2012 when I interviewed to become Brian Butler's partner (first as his assistant principal, and ultimately as his co-principal) in opening a brand-new elementary school in Annandale, Virginia. The stars aligned and I was lucky to be offered the job. At that point we embarked on what turned out to be the most rewarding working partnership I have ever had. I learned an incredible amount both from and with Brian. In him I found a partner with similar beliefs on education and gained a lifelong friend.

Opening a new school is a once-in-a-lifetime experience that few people have the honor to do. At the outset there were many tasks required, from hiring staff to buying furniture. One of the most important actions we took was taking some of our early hired staff on a retreat with Rick and Becky DuFour. During that retreat we developed our mission, vision, and collective commitments for our brand-new school. These would serve as a foundation for our school, and they guided our daily work. It turns out that our mission, "ensuring high levels of learning for all students and adults," was the seed that sprouted into the idea that gifted education should be for *all* students.

While striving to create a learning environment that would promote high levels of learning for all, we were forced to wrestle with the traditional system of gifted education—a system that promoted special curricula and learning opportunities for a select few. This antiquated system was absolutely contrary to our mission. We could and did do better. This book includes the story of how we developed our new school. As is true of most journeys worth taking, ours was bumpy and we often took some side trips. However, it is the failures and successes in doing this work, Brian's drive to advocate for all students, and his decades of experience that make this book credible—and one I desperately hope many will read.

What I enjoy most about this book is how Brian balances *why* we must think and do differently with respect to "gifted" learning with *how* to make it happen. He expertly weaves stories from other successful educators with his own examples to make a wonderfully compelling read. Additionally, he provides opportunities during each chapter to reflect on your reading and apply that learning to your current reality.

When you read this book, please do not skip the introduction. It sets the stage for why we must approach gifted education differently. As you move through the chapters, I encourage you to study the evidence provided and reflect on your own beliefs about intelligence, mindset, and attaching labels to students (chapters 1 and 2). The next two chapters focus on collaboration and collective teacher efficacy as the force behind the work in classrooms while providing instructional strategies that can be learned and used immediately. The last chapter provides great examples of addressing resistance, since there will be nonbelievers and people who are not yet ready to embrace this change. Lastly, a special talent of Brian's is his ability to motivate and inspire those around him. He does so throughout the book and brings his message home in the last chapter.

This book screams everything that I know to be true about Brian's advocacy for students, families, and educators. He is fiercely committed to doing the right thing for students—not necessarily the most popular or trendy thing, but what is right. Choosing to do what is right is what this book is all about. Making gifted education available to *all* students is truly the right thing to do. After reading this book, I venture to guess that you too will be inspired to at least dip your toe into this sea of possibilities and do the right thing as an educator.

Diane Kerr
Author and Educational Consultant

Introduction

"The lesson here is very simple. But it is striking how often it is over-looked. We are so caught in the myths of the best and the brightest and the self-made that we think outliers spring naturally from the earth. We look at the young Bill Gates and marvel that our world allowed that thirteen-year-old to become a fabulously successful entrepreneur. But that's the wrong lesson. Our world only allowed one thirteen-year-old unlimited access to a time-sharing terminal in 1968. If a million teen-agers had been given the same opportunity, how many more Microsofts would we have today? To build a better world we need to replace the patchwork of lucky breaks and arbitrary advantages that determine success—fortunate birth dates and happy accidents of history—with a society that provides opportunities for all."

—MALCOLM GLADWELL[1]

The Wrong Question

The traditional idea of gifted education has supported this myth of the Bell Curve, supremacy, or a caste system in our schools. We have continued to ask the wrong questions regarding gifted education. We keep asking, *"How do we get more kids of color, school-dependent kids, and English Language Learners into Gifted Programs?"* **That's the wrong question!** We should ask, *"How do we create the conditions,*

---

1. Gladwell, Malcolm, *Outliers*, Little, Brown and Company, 2008.

expectations, beliefs, and mindset so that all schools can give each student a gifted education? How can we recognize the genius, awaken the genius, and cultivate the genius in every child?"

You will notice that I used the pronoun **we** in the above questions. Why? Because it will take the teacher teams in a school to pull this off for every child. Of course, an individual teacher can have the belief and high expectations that all students have the capacity for high intellectual performance, but to do away with the educational lottery for kids, ("the luck of the draw," kids might say, or "I was lucky enough to get the teacher who believed that all kids can learn at high levels") and to make it systematic, the team's collective efficacy and collective responsibility for each student will ensure that a gifted experience for every child comes to fruition. But sure enough, it will take each educator's fearless belief, expectations, and confidence to pull this off!

I am going to begin with a challenge to the reader. My challenge to you is to wipe the slate clean and to be open to viewing Gifted Education (also known as Advanced Academics in some districts) through new eyes. These new eyes should see Gifted Education as our FLOOR, accessible to all and not just a select, fortunate few. Old and new research supports the position that all students have the capacity for high intellectual performance. We've just turned a blind eye to it, ignored it, or outright disregarded the research. The following quotes from prominent researchers, authors, or experts in the field support the contention:

"The new science of genetics, intelligence, and talent suggests that our abilities are not set in genetic stone, but rather are soft and sculptable. People are not doomed to mediocrity, as conventional wisdom suggests. No one can really know his or her true limits before applying enormous resources and investing vast amounts of time. Greatness is something to which any kid—of any age—can aspire."[2]

2. Schulten, Katherine, "Does the 'Gifted' Label Get In the Way of Developing Real Potential?" David Shenk, *The New York Times*, March 12, 2010. https://archive.nytimes.com/learning.blogs.nytimes.com/2010/03/12/teacher-q-does-the-gifted-label-get-in-the-way-of-developing-real-potential/

"...having been the director of Gifted Programs in a district as large and diverse as New York City, I found that gifted education is a pedagogical resource we can learn from to guide education of ALL students. The philosophy of gifted education is what ALL parents want for their children. And our country would benefit if we offered to ALL students what gifted education currently provides to only a few—pedagogy that elicits high intellectual performance to motivate self-directed learning and self-actualization."[3]

"Further, when lower-performing students experience curriculum and instruction focused on meaning and understanding, they increase their skills at least as much as their higher-achieving peers do (Educational Research Service, 1992)....Virtually all students would benefit from the kind of curriculum and instruction we have often reserved for advanced learners—that is, curriculum and instruction designed to engage students, with a focus on meaning making, problem solving, logical thinking, and transfer of learning."[4]

This Book Is Not for Everybody.
So, Who Is This Book Written For?

This book is for educators, administrators, and school and district leaders who...

...are willing to examine the brutal facts of their current reality and some of their own beliefs and practices that are not aligned with gifted education for all.

...are passionate and embrace the idea of continuous improvement.

---

3. Jackson, Yvette, *The Pedagogy of Confidence*, Teachers College Press, 2011, p. 87.

4. Tomlinson, Carol Ann and Javius, Edwin Lou, "For Each to Excel: Teach Up for Excellence," *Educational Leadership*, 69(5), February 1, 2012, 28-33, https://www.ascd.org/el/articles/teach-up-for-excellence.

...are willing to take collective responsibility for every student on their team, in their school, and/or in their district.

...have fearless expectations and support for all students to demonstrate high intellectual performance.

...are fiercely optimistic—no Eeyores. If you believe it's going to work, it will.

...are willing to examine their language and abandon negative labels.

...are willing to embrace new effective practices and abandon old ineffective practices.

...must be willing to challenge the systems and prevailing mindset regarding traditional gifted education. People and systems will push back, and you must be willing to go it alone as a team, a school, or a district in the face of the pressure to hold on to the status quo.

You might be disappointed if you expect this to be a traditional education book. This book focuses on culture, individual and collective beliefs, and expectations. I did not intend to write about curriculum, instruction, assessments, and interventions, as there are already numerous valuable books on those subjects. However, with a solid foundation for teachers and students to rely on, which fosters the belief among adults in schools that all students deserve a gifted education, the effectiveness of the best curriculum, instruction, assessment, and intervention practices becomes relevant.

How Did We Get Here?

This book is not about the traditional definition and approach to *gifted education*. However, we will begin with some background about the *traditional definition and approach to gifted education* to move forward with

a different definition and approach. This new definition and approach centers around the belief that we can make Gifted Education Practices & Strategies the Floor to Every Classroom. We can make it a reality for every student we expect to be an independent adult when they leave the Pre-K-12 school system. Let's start by assuming *all* kids can learn at high levels and we, as adults, will help them discover the unique strengths, passions, and talents that they will take and turn into something special, a gift.

An entire review of the history, issues, and intricacies of gifted education is not the purpose of this book and is beyond its scope. However, it is important to provide some historical context on how we arrived at traditional Gifted Education and how it is viewed and implemented in schools today.

In researching the definition of Gifted and Talented, I found varying definitions of the term. Erin McIntyre supported my assertion by writing, *"No blanket definition of 'giftedness' exists across states or local education agencies. And no existing national requirements guide how gifted programs are executed."*[5]

In fact, in New York City schools the definition of gifted education starts with this qualifying statement: **"Nearly every state in the country has its own definition of giftedness."** Then they go on to define gifted students in this way. *"The current New York State definition is as follows: 'Gifted pupils are those who show evidence of high-performance capability and exceptional potential in areas such as general intellectual ability, special academic aptitude, and outstanding ability in visual and performing arts. Such definition shall include those pupils who require educational programs or services beyond those normally provided by the regular school program to realize their full potential.'" Do you notice that the definition says "current," meaning it could change?*[6]

---

5. McIntyre, Erin, "Minorities, low-income kids underrepresented among gifted students," K-12dive, November 2, 2015, https://www.k12dive.com/news/minorities-low-income-kids-underrepresented-among-gifted-students/408365/.

6. "What is Gifted?" GiftedNYS, https://giftednys.org/resources/what-is-gifted/#:~:text=New%20York%20State%20Definition&text=%E2%80%9CGifted%20pupils%20are%20those%20who,in%20visual%20and%20performing%20arts.

In her book *The Pedagogy of Confidence*, Yvette Jackson shares that the idea of "gifted programs" resulted from the United States' competition with Russia because of the launch of Sputnik (the world's first Earth-orbiting artificial satellite). She said that it spurred the U.S. to focus on mathematics and science to compete for dominance with Russia and sparked a need to identify students early on who might be considered to have exceptional abilities. To promote this idea, Jackson wrote that the federal government created five categories in which students could be considered gifted (creative or productive thinking, visual or performing arts, leadership, academic aptitude, and general intellectual ability), and funding was allotted accordingly.[7]

On a Tom Schimmer podcast in 2021, Jackson said that the government considered a sixth category of giftedness, sports, but decided against it because it would cost too much. She added, "The government said 3-5 percent we are going to label as gifted. Now why that? Because they figured by giving a statistic, a range of 3-5 percent…they could limit how much money they would allow. People interpreted that as only 3-5 percent of the population is gifted. That is totally empirically not true. They never did any kind of testing at all."[8]

In 2009, James Borland addressed the misconception of 3%-5% of the population being gifted in his article "Myth 2: The Gifted Constitute 3%-5% of the Population." He noted that despite this myth being debunked by people like Joseph Renzulli in *Gifted Quarterly* back in 1982, it continues to persist, appearing resistant to rationality and experiential lessons. He went on to say that "giftedness is not a fact of nature but, instead, a social construction and the notion of a certain percentage of the population being gifted

7. Jackson, Yvette, *The Pedagogy of Confidence*, Teachers College Press, 2011.

8. "With Age Comes…," The Tom Schimmer Podcast, PodBean, May 10, 2021, https://www.podbean.com/ew/pb-55bti-1031776.

as a matter of empirically verifiable fact is logically incoherent."[9]

Earlier in my career, I found myself sharing this fallacy as well. I heard a fellow seasoned educator say that only 3% of the student population was gifted, and for years I would say the same thing. It is so interesting that many among us in education have repeated such fallacies so often that they become "truths" in our minds, directly affecting our beliefs, psyche, actions, programs, and policies.

In 1977, Lynn Hasher, David Goldstein, and Thomas Toppino conducted a groundbreaking study that explored the human "tendency to believe false information to be correct after repeated exposure." They coined this phenomenon the "illusory truth effect" or the "reiteration effect." The study revealed that when something is said repeatedly and without fact-checking, it can create a false truth akin to a fallacy or myth.[10]

Marshall Shepherd (2020) addressed this significant finding in his article "Repeating Misinformation Doesn't Make It True, But Does Make It More Likely To Be Believed." He asserted that professionals in marketing, cult leadership, and politics understand the power of repetition in shaping beliefs—the more a statement is reiterated, the more likely people are to believe it. Shepherd went on to share that Dr. Joe Pierre, writing in *Psychology Today*, brought forth additional characteristics of this effect, including the notion that if the information is repeated frequently enough, it may be perceived as true, even when the sources are not credible.[11]

9. Borland, James, "Myth 2: The Gifted Constitute 3%-5% of the Population," *Gifted Child Quarterly* 53(4), September 2009, pp. 236-238, https://www.researchgate.net/publication/249827570_Myth_2_The_Gifted_Constitute_3_to_5_of_the_Population_Moreover_Giftedness_Equals_High_IQ_Which_Is_a_Stable_Measure_of_AptitudeSpinal_Tap_Psychometrics_in_Gifted_Education.

10. Hasher, Lynn, Goldstein, David, and Toppino, Thomas, "Frequency and the conference of referential validity," *Journal of Verbal Learning and Verbal Behavior* 16 (1), February 1977, pp. 107-112.

11. Shepherd, Marshall, "Repeating Misinformation Doesn't Make It True, But Does Make It More Likely To Be Believed," *Forbes*, August 17, 2020, https://www.forbes.com/sites/marshallshepherd/2020/08/17/why-repeating-false-science-information-doesnt-make-it-true/?sh=2dcc20171ffd.

Emphasizing Yvette Jackson's assertion once more, there is no credible empirical support for the claim that 3%-5% of the population is gifted. As she unequivocally stated on the Tom Schimmer Podcast in 2021, "There is absolutely no empirical basis for this assertion. No testing has ever been conducted to establish the percentage of gifted individuals in our population."[12]

This leads me to wonder how many beliefs in education have not been debunked because we have chosen not to use research and evidence but instead we heard it and repeated it as the illusory truth effect demonstrates. A common belief immediately comes to mind is the myth that people are born intelligent, and their intelligence can't change much.

Recent insights into human cognition have revealed the remarkable adaptability of our brains, challenging the notion of fixed intelligence. This principle is highlighted in Carol Dweck's groundbreaking 2006 book *Mindset*, in which she explores the concept of a "growth mindset." This mindset emphasizes that our abilities and intelligence can be developed through effort and challenges, a concept we will explore in Chapter 1. By embracing this perspective, we unlock the door for continuous self-improvement and a deeper appreciation for the brain's transformative capabilities.[13]

More importantly, how many other fallacies do we hold onto that have yet to be debunked? This fallacy or confusion around who is "gifted," combined with the fact that gifted programs have not benefitted all students and groups equally, has left many to wonder about the fairness of the process for identifying gifted and talented students.

As more and more school systems integrated in the 1970s, a phenomenon occurred among a particular segment of the population called "white flight." In her article "Ending Racial Inequality in Gifted Education," Sarah Garland wrote:

12. With Age Comes...," The Tom Schimmer Podcast, PodBean, May 10, 2021, https://www.podbean.com/ew/pb-55bti-1031776.

13. Dweck, C. S. *Mindset*, Ballantine Books, 2008.

"...in the 1970s as huge demographic changes were transforming urban school districts, white, middle-class families were fleeing to the suburbs. Like magnet schools, accelerated programs for gifted students were attractive to many of these families and provided a way to counteract this flight and maintain diversity in city school systems. The problem was that gifted programs tended to foster racial separation inside schools, undermining the goal they were supposed to support. Today, gifted programs still tend to separate students by race." She went on to state that "determining whether a child is more intelligent than her peers or whether she's just the product of more affluent, ambitious parents is a difficult task for school systems interested in breaking the cycle of privilege that gifted education tends to fuel. Experts caution against relying heavily on tests...but there are no national or even state standards defining giftedness, according to the National Society for the Gifted and Talented, an advocacy group."[14]

This was the case in a district I formerly worked in. Out of the fear of white flight, the school district created Gifted /Advanced Academics Centers for students who performed well on entrance tests. Having worked there, I have no doubt it's a system with outstanding educators with many great things going on. But employees don't make policy. In my opinion the school board continues through this policy to embrace **the illusory truth effect**. Although through words they may say otherwise, the school board, through its actions or inaction, by keeping the symbol of the 1970s in place, has held on to the myth that only some students deserve a gifted experience and must be separated from their peers to achieve this goal. I can't remember any principal or teacher in conversations while I worked in that district ever being in favor of keeping these centers.

---

14. Garland, Sarah, "Ending Racial Inequality in Gifted Education," Hechinger Report, March 14, 2013, https://hechingerreport.org/ending-racial-inequality-in-gifted-education.

Beth English, a retired principal from that same district, shared with me some of her thoughts and experiences as the principal of a school that housed the Gifted/Advanced Academics Centers and a separate school within the building of "students who were not identified" to attend the center. Here are some excerpts of what Beth shared in our conversation (2023):

> "The most heartbreaking part for me was when children would tell me, "Dr. English, I must be stupid. I'm not in the center." I had to say, "Oh honey, please, you are very smart. It has nothing to do with intelligence—it has to do with the test."
>
> On the day when the children from other schools who got into the (Gifted/AA) center at my school get invited to come to orientation and the children in the second grade at my school who didn't qualify for the center in third grade have to stay behind and watch their classmates, the selected ones go to the orientation with all these children who are coming from other schools. I mean, it's heartbreaking.
>
> Now I see these children being in a center; it did nothing for them academically, obviously, and I believe it did much harm to them emotionally. Whether you were in a center or not in a center, you were separated from and denied access to other children, whom you shouldn't have been separated from.[15]

What did you think about what Beth shared? What words and thoughts immediately came to your mind as she discussed the different student experiences? Please take a moment and write your thoughts and reflections in the space below.

---

15. English, Beth, personal communication, May 15, 2023.

Confronting the Brutal Truths of Our Current Reality

"MR. BUTLER, WHERE IS THE 'SMART CLASS' THAT I AM SUPPOSED TO BE IN?"

I can remember it as if it was yesterday, although it was more than a decade ago at Mason Crest Elementary School, a school with kids who spoke 35 languages and came from 40 countries at the time. Our new school had an open house before the beginning of the school year to welcome students and parents to meet their new Teacher Team. Yes, you read that right, their "Teacher Team." Although students would be assigned to a teacher, we explained to students and parents that they would enjoy the benefits of each teacher's knowledge, skills, wisdom, experience, and expertise as they worked with that grade level.

As parents and students entered the school at the beginning of the open house, I and other staff greeted them. One student approached me with his parents behind him and asked, "Are you the principal?" I said yes, told him my name, asked him his name, and shook his hand. His next words took me aback. His question was: **"Where is the smart class that I am supposed to be in?"**

Here is where I must give some background about the school system where I worked. I do not mean to disparage the great educators in that system because they were good, decent, hard-working people who cared deeply about the students' success. What I have found is that you can put great people in a traditional system and more times than not they will conform to that system and be team players, even if it's clear as the nose on one's face that the system does not benefit each student equally.

In the school system in which I worked at the time, students could be identified to receive what is traditionally known as "gifted service" or "advanced academics" by taking a test, putting together a portfolio, and receiving a teacher recommendation. There were four levels in which students could receive these services, but the "golden ticket" was for a student to be identified as Level IV, which meant that they then had the option of going to a separate building away from their home elementary school, or even be separated within their home school, with other students with a Level IV designation. The other benefit of this label was that it gave students automatic entry into the middle school "Advanced Academics Center."

Sharon Santos, a staff writer for *The Purple Tide*, a high school newspaper, wrote an opinion piece about the inequities of Fairfax County's Advanced Academic Program and noted that African American and Hispanic students are underrepresented in Level 4 Advanced Academics Programs. Sharon, who is Hispanic, wrote this piece as a student who was able to attend a Level IV Advanced Academics Center. Although she was in the center, she knew something wasn't right when she arrived in third grade. Here is what she said:

"In third grade, I transferred to a new school to join an elite class of 'advanced' students. My base school had a large Hispanic population. Despite my new school also having a large Hispanic population, my class was strikingly different in terms of demographics with most students being white or Asian-American. As one of the few Hispanic students, I felt something was very wrong. I see now that this separation is all too like the overt segregation that continues to plague this nation."

Sharon concluded, "The solution does not lie in funding the programs that separate students based on test scores and other subjective metrics collected when the student is between seven and eight years old and guarantees them access to an elite class until high school. The solution lies in assuring each child has what they need to achieve their academic potential."[16]

I will stop now and ask you to think about the term "label," which we will address in detail in Chapter 2. Labeling, in my opinion, has been one of the most damaging things we do in education because it changes expectations depending on the label and takes us away from genuinely teaching each student and their unique needs, strengths, passions, and talents. Labeling has been a source of separating and sorting students,

---

16. Santos, Sharon, "FCPS' AAP Program Inherently Racist, classist...," *The Purple Tide*, March 19, 2022, https://chantillynews.org/9790/opinions/fcps-aap-program-inherently-racist-classist.

benefiting only a few. When reflecting on the title of the book and this idea of labeling, consider the following:

Carol Ann Tomlinson and Edwin Lou Javius wrote, *"Research finds that sorting, this 21st-century version of school segregation, correlates strongly with student race and economic status and predicts and contributes to student outcomes, with students in higher-level classes typically experiencing better teachers, curriculum, and achievement levels than peers in lower-level classes."*[17]

In her article "There Is Actually No Such Thing As a Gifted Child," Karishma Sarkari cited Wendy Berliner, co-author of *Great Minds and How to Grow Them,* "with supportive and encouraging learning environments the average child can perform just as well or better than one believed to be 'gifted.'"[18]

Angel de Dios shared on his blog: *"To appreciate why Gifted Talented programs contribute to inequity in education, one must simply acknowledge that quality education and learning opportunities are being provided only to a few that have been selected based on their parent's educational attainment and income. This happens because identification and segregation are done very early in a child's basic education. There is no flexibility as children become labeled. Resources (not so much in terms of quantity but more on quality) are diverted to the education of the selected children of privilege.*[19]

---

17. Tomlinson, C. A. and Javius, E. L., "For Each to Excel: Teach Up for Excellence," *Educational Leadership,* 69(5), February 1, 2012, pp. 28-33, https://www.ascd.org/el/articles/teach-up-for-excellence.

18. Sarkarmi, Karishma, "New study Says There Is Actually No Such Thing As a Gifted Child," Kidspot, July 26, 2017, https://www.kidspot.com.au/parenting/real-life/in-the-news/new-study-says-there-is actually-no-such-thing-as-a-gifted-child/news-story/f7e8b1b63955e0321b481fefd0b7c4db.

19. de Dios, Angel, "Equity Is Not Reducing Schools to the Lowest Common Denominator," Philippine Basic Education, October 10, 2019, https://www.philippinesbasiceducation.us/2019/10/equity-is-not-reducing-schools-to.html.

Born in the Right Family

Our education system has shown bias against students who may not have had the advantage of being born into a privileged family. I mention this not to criticize parents, as they strive to ensure their children's success. However, I've witnessed parents go to extreme lengths to secure their child's admission into a gifted program, even resorting to purchasing test materials or completing portfolios on their behalf. Portfolios, which students can complete at home, are used to demonstrate their eligibility for advanced designation.

Now, let's consider other situations where parents assist their children, such as with homework. Many of us, including my wife and me, have helped our children with homework to varying extents. Yet, this practice raises concerns when it comes to grading. Students who lack parental guidance are put at a clear disadvantage.

Reflecting on my own experience, early struggles in reading highlighted the role of family support. My parents attended college, and my father, a reading teacher, helped me catch up. This support and enriching experiences ensured I had a solid comprehension background despite initial reading difficulties.

The concept of being born into the "right family" isn't a matter of judgment but rather a matter of chance. Throughout my years, I've witnessed that all parents love and desire the best for their children irrespective of background. Nevertheless, time, energy, expertise, and knowledge disparities can hinder a parent's ability to supplement school teachings at home. This disconnect can sometimes blur the lines between parental involvement and the actual achievement of the student.

A personal anecdote from fourth grade exemplifies this perfectly. Tasked with constructing a historical structure, I procrastinated and sought last-minute parental intervention. My father ultimately took charge of the project, resulting in an impressive castle. Though I had limited direct involvement, my dad's efforts earned a B grade. This incident underscores how a student's home environment can significantly shape academic achievements. What if I was born into a different family without the kind of support my parents were able to provide?

As an educator, I understand that the quality of work at home often reflects parental assistance, which can affect grades and even acceptance into a "Gifted Program." While parents act out of love, we must question the validity of outcomes, especially when completed at home. This prompts a vital evaluation of fairness, especially when comparing students with varying degrees of parental support.

Let's get back to the students who asked, **"Where is the 'smart class' that I am supposed to be in?"** As I noted earlier, students with the designation of Level IV Gifted/Advanced Academics label got to choose to attend what was called the "Advanced Academics Center," a separate building away from their home school or a separate program within their school if their school was one of the designated centers. To mitigate the flight of students who had the Level IV designation from their home schools, the county said that home schools that were not designated Advanced Academic Centers could create special classes within their school made up of Level IV students as well as Level III students if the class was not full and possibly other students who teachers "deemed worthy" of being able to handle the class. Sounds great, right?

Creative Insubordination

Do you remember at the beginning when I said you could put great people in a traditional system, and more times than not they will conform to that system and be "team players" even if it's clear as the nose on one's face that the system does not benefit each student equally? Stay with me... In opening a new school where we were getting students from four other schools because of overcrowding, we truly believed that we could educate any student, but we made a mistake. We agreed to be a "traditional local Level IV" site in which we placed all the students who had the Level IV designation in their separate classes and filled in the class with students who had the Level III designation and a few others from recommendations from their teachers from their sending schools.

Our actions on this issue did not match our words. We were creating a caste system within our school, which was wrong. Two things made us look in the mirror and see our "nose" clearly.

Why Do They Get to Go to the "Smart Class"?

The first ton of bricks that hit my heart more than anything was when students started asking us, **"Why do they get to go to the 'smart class'?"** Our students could see the inequity of sorting and selecting, bias, and lowering expectations just by the location of who was in what class. I knew at that moment that we had conformed to the traditional system and we had lost our moral high ground to an extent. How can we tell students they are unique and have unlimited potential to learn at high levels when we show them that only some do by the class they attend?

The second ton of bricks came from Hannah and Jessie, who came to the administration and communicated how wrong this was. Hannah Aldridge and Jessica Bagnall are two of the most outstanding educators and human beings I have ever been around. They came with me to help open our new school, Mason Crest, from my previous school, Mount Eagle, another school where we helped to achieve International Model Professional Learning Communities at Work status.

Let's digress for a quick but important detail about Mount Eagle, my first school as principal. The school district wanted to give students from underrepresented groups access to advanced academic services by creating a special category called "Young Scholars." Sounds great and noble, correct? Giving more access to students who traditionally have not had access sounds like a worthy ideal, but my question immediately was, which one is worthy? And what student does not deserve access to a "gifted experience"? The district had said we had to be a part of this, and to me, it was a bit of a guilt trip because if not, we were denying underrepresented children a chance to participate in something they would not have without this designation of "Young Scholar." So, I took a page from our courageous superintendent at the time, Dr. Jack Dale, who told all administrators at a meeting that the traditional system wouldn't change itself in education, so he challenged the administrators in the district "to be creatively insubordinate."

So creatively insubordinate we were! I wasn't about to subject the students at Mount Eagle to a "Young Scholars" lottery, in which the underrepresented student who fit the profile (whatever profile we deemed worthy) would get the golden ticket as a Young Scholar. So, what did we do? They didn't tell us we had to have a certain number of Young Scholars; the district just said each school had to identify "these diamonds in the rough." So, I said code them all! What, Brian? I said to our staff person who did the category coding of who was a Young Scholar in the computer that every student in our building would be coded as a Young Scholar! Creative insubordination! It would be our job as educators in the building to create the belief, expectations, and practices to treat each child as the unique geniuses that they were.

Hannah and Jessie were with me at Mount Eagle as fourth-grade teachers. They were as good a teacher team as I have ever experienced because of their passion, transparency, and willingness to continuously improve on behalf of our students. They also were willing to confront their principal, me, if we were not honoring our mission and walking our talk. As I shared, when I went to open Mason Crest, I knew I needed Hannah and Jessie to be a part of it.

Sometime during our first year, Hannah and Jessie came to me and said: Brian, this doesn't seem right. Having designated Level IV classes here at Mason Crest is everything you are against, and it's not how we operated at Mount Eagle. They were correct, and I knew it. I, me—yes, me Brian Butler—had allowed the system to pressure me to conform and to go against my core belief that each child has a gift and is unique. Labeling and sorting and selecting students based on "traditional methods" of identifying "who has got it, and who doesn't" is not only wrong but it hurts all students. Hannah and Jessie were the first, but then the floodgates opened of staff members voicing their concern about our "local Level IV" separate classes. They knew, and we—meaning Diane Kerr, my co-principal, and I—knew we had to do better and would.

As a staff, we continued to learn together around the research and gifted practices we would promise to all students, no matter the label. We disbanded the Level IV classes (not the services) in our second year and never looked back (see MCES Evolution Below).

We intentionally built time to learn together throughout the year and before school started in our pre-service workdays, during our staff early-release days, and during our teacher team-planning meetings.

Traditional AAP Class:	Mason Crest '12–'13:	Mason Crest '13–'14:
Only students eligible for level 4 services; Limited interaction with other grade level peers	Students eligible for level 4 services and students with potential for advanced academics; Limited interaction with other grade level peers	Students will be strategically grouped into homerooms with more interaction with grade level peers in some content areas, specials, and lunch/recess
1 teacher working in isolation to plan instruction for the 4 core areas	1 teacher working in isolation to plan for advanced math instruction with support from math specialist and AART	Multiple teachers working together to plan advanced math instruction with support from math specialist and AART
Students expected to have mastery of 3rd grade math curriculum in order to move directly to 4th grade math curriculum	Students access grade level above math standards when they show mastery of current grade level standards	Students access grade level above math standards when they show mastery of current grade level standards
Limited interaction with the Advanced Academics, Reading, Math, and Technology Specialists	Common team planning for Language Arts, Social Studies, and Science with students' needs being met by differentiation	Common team planning for Language Arts, Social Studies, and Science with students' needs being met by differentiation
Access to William and Mary Units, Jacob's Ladder, M3, Socratic Seminar	Jacob's Ladder, M3, Socratic Seminar, Groundworks	Jacob's Ladder, M3, Socratic Seminar, William and Mary Units, Groundworks
Instruction moves at a quicker pace and goes more in depth	Instruction moves at a quicker pace and goes more in depth	Instruction moves at a quicker pace and goes more in depth
Global Themes that cross curricular areas and cultures		Global Themes that cross curricular areas and cultures
Project based learning experiences with students strategically grouped		Integration of content areas through project based learning experiences with students strategically grouped

The learning of all students skyrocketed, and the authentic culture and climate improved because only then did Mason Crest become a "We" school. To be frank, I didn't want to know the Advanced Academics label of students. It didn't matter to me. We would give each child what they needed, kid by kid, skill by skill, based on our formative assessment system and our frequent checks for understanding.

We also did something that no other school I knew of at the time was doing. Most schools had an Advanced Academics Resource Teacher (AART), whose traditional job was to focus on the Level IV classes and some scant support from other students and teachers. Morgan Huynh was our AART, and this is how Morgan described her job at Mason Crest:

> Fairfax County schools have four levels of advanced academic services. All students receive level I services in the form of Critical & Creative Thinking Lessons. Level II services refer to extension in a particular subject area, achieved through Advanced Academic Program (AAP) curriculum lessons. Level III services indicate that a student is eligible for part-time AAP services. These are traditionally provided by the Advanced Academic Resource Teacher (AART), who may pull small groups to work on extension or enrichment in different subject areas. Level IV services refer to the full-time advanced academic program, which can be a school-based or center program.
>
> When I started my role as the AART at Mason Crest, we were a Local Level IV school-based program, meaning that students could opt to stay at Mason Crest for full-time advanced academic services in grades 3-5. Early on I asked our principals, Brian Butler and Diane Kerr, how they would like me to proceed as the AART at Mason Crest. They responded, "Figure it out!" and "You have to be comfortable with the uncomfortable." They did not expect me to be the resident expert on gifted education. Instead, they saw me as a resource to assist teacher teams

with differentiating the curriculum to ensure all students were appropriately challenged.

While Brian and Diane entrusted me with defining the role of the AART at Mason Crest, they communicated certain principles that helped guide that decision-making process. Brian and Diane asked that I participate in all planning meetings for math and language arts for third through fifth grade weekly. I needed to be an integral part of each team and be able to assist with vertical articulation across grade levels. It was also important that we met all students where they were academically across the curriculum, rather than labeling them and providing set extensions solely based on their "advanced academic level." A final defining principle was that all teachers had the ability to provide both support and extension. Since our planning meetings included ESOL (English Language) teachers, special education teachers, classroom teachers, reading and math specialists, and myself, we were able to share best practices for supporting students across all levels.

As the AART at Mason Crest, I never pulled isolated groups related to a level of service. I did meet with small groups, but always in a strategic way that related directly to the instruction happening in the classroom. It was important in our weekly planning meetings to put together shared, intentional plans for the week. The teachers understood that the instruction taking place in the classroom was the most important instruction the students could be receiving. Rather than pulling students out of that instruction to teach a separate curriculum, our specialists, I included, often pushed into the classroom to assist in differentiation through a co-teaching model.

Because we shared all our students and were flexible throughout the year, we were able to ensure that students regularly received extensions when needed. A student was never denied extension or access to a particular curriculum because of their defined level of AAP service.[20]

---

20. Huynh, Morgan, personal communication (email), May 17, 2023.

"How we use the word 'gifted' itself points to an underlying problem in the field. Once it is deprived of the aura that surrounds its use, what does the term 'gifted' convey practically? The word is often used either to refer to a fixed state of being ('She is gifted') or to high potential in a particular area of human performance, usually in comparison to a set criterion or group ('He is a gifted writer for his age'). These two different interpretations of the term "gifted" raise what might be the most important questions: Is one born gifted, or are gifted behaviors developmental? And can we develop these behaviors in larger numbers of students than those who are the highest scorers on cognitive ability or academic achievement tests?"[21]

About Now, I Can Imagine a Few of You Saying, "Yeah, but Brian..."

Here are a few reactions that I have heard:

We can't do this because too many students don't have a gifted label. This is only for gifted students.

We can't do this because we are already too busy.

We can't do this because we don't have the resources.

We can't do this because the parents of the students with a "gifted label" want their child in a separate class.

We can't do this because our colleagues, district, and super-intendent won't go for it.

We can't do this because you know some kids are just "smarter" than others and that's just the way it is.

---

21. Renzulli, Joseph S., "What We're Getting Wrong About Gifted Education," EducationWeek, November 11, 2019, https://www.edweek.org/teaching-learning/opinion-what-were-getting-wrong-about-gifted-education/2019/11.

We can't do this because we will get in trouble by treating each kid as if they had a gift. (Yes, this was said!)

We can't do this because we have too many English Learners.

We can't do this because there will always be a Bell Curve.

We can't do this because it's watering down our expectations.

We can't do this because you know only 3%-5% of students are gifted! Everyone can't be gifted!

We can't do this because parents of high-achieving early bloomers will have a fit.

The traditional approach to gifted education caters to a select few, while my approach aims to provide gifted experiences for all students. My primary objective is to utilize our understanding of the fallacy of fixed intelligence and challenge the misconception that only specific students deserve a gifted and challenging educational experience. I am dedicated to working with educators to change their expectations and beliefs, fostering competence and confidence within them, and nurturing each student's unique strengths, passions, and talents.

Our collective objective is to establish schools that grant equal opportunities to every student. The focus is to provide practices that meet a minimum standard known as "THE FLOOR," aligning with what is currently offered to students who have been identified as gifted. Importantly, these practices have demonstrated positive outcomes for all students, transcending the exclusive boundaries of the gifted label.

"How will we maintain the ambition of those showing early promise," asked author David Shenk, "while simultaneously trying to tap into and nurture the hidden potential of everyone else?"[22]

22. Schulten, Katherine, "Does the 'Gifted' Label Get In the Way of Developing Real Potential?" *The New York Times*, March 12, 2010, https://archive.nytimes.com/learning.blogs.nytimes.com/2010/03/12/teacher-q-does-the-gifted-label-get-in-the-way-of-developing-real-potential/.

Read on!

Educators, it is our moral obligation to have the exact expectations of the children we serve in schools as we do for our children or a child who is special to us in our personal lives! I contend that it's our moral obligation to challenge the status quo to match our actions with our words. *Every Student Deserves a Gifted Education—The 5 Shifts to Nurturing Each Student's Unique Strengths, Passions, and Talents* will create the solid FLOOR to make our promise a reality.

In the following five chapters, you will learn how to make this a reality. Each chapter will address a letter in the acronym **FLOOR**.

Chapter Overviews

In Chapter 1, titled "**F** = Fallacy of Fixed Intelligence," the reader is introduced to the research on the brain, the science of learning, and the growth mindset belief that dispels the myth of fixed intelligence. This chapter can be likened to a room's initial cleaning and preparation before painting. By building shared knowledge about the brain and learning, the reader is ensured a basic understanding of the subject matter, just as cleaning the room creates a clean and blank canvas for the painting.

Chapter 2, "**L** = Labels Be Gone," explores the harmful effects of marginalizing labels and offers strategies to mitigate their impact on beliefs, expectations, and actions. This chapter can be likened to sanding and patching the walls before painting. By examining the harmful effects of labels and providing ways to overcome them, I smooth out any rough patches in readers' understanding, preparing you for the transformative journey ahead.

In Chapter 3, "**O** = Obligation of Teams," I emphasize the power of collective teacher efficacy and collective responsibility, encouraging educators to embrace vulnerability and transparency to ensure that the sum becomes greater than its parts. This chapter can be compared to priming the walls before painting, as it creates a receptive and supportive environment for educator growth and learning. Just as priming prepares the walls to absorb better and showcase the paint, Chapter 3 sets the stage for educators to collaborate and leverage their collective expertise, enhancing the educational experience for all students.

By taking the time to establish these crucial foundational chapters—1, 2, and 3—readers are equipped with the necessary knowledge and mindset to engage with the subsequent chapters thoroughly.

Chapter 4, "**O** = Our Superpowers," identifies seven powerful strategies educators can use to create a dynamic and enriching learning environment. In this chapter, we will explore how teacher teams can apply these superpowers to unlock the unlimited potential of their students. The second part of the chapter will also focus on gifting students with seven attributes or superpowers and various aspects of personal habits to develop that contribute to overall well-being and success.

Chapter 5, titled "**R** = Resistance & Inspiration," has two sections. The first section addresses the challenge of resistance to change, which can be difficult within an organization's culture. People often resist and oppose change due to various logical and illogical factors. This section provides strategies to navigate through the change process successfully.

The second part of the chapter focuses on drawing inspiration from the success of others in educational settings and individuals who have overcome challenges to share their gifts with the world. The achievements of others can serve as a powerful catalyst. Witnessing someone accomplish what may seem difficult or impossible, overcoming obstacles, serves as a reminder of what is achievable and can ignite motivation within us. By observing others embrace the mindset shift that "Every Child Deserves a Gifted Education," we hope to change the perspective of those who may be unsure or skeptical.

Just as the final chapters, 4 and 5, of the book are the equivalent of the painting process itself, the intention is for readers to apply the insights gained from the earlier chapters and experience the true power of the book's core messages of *Nurturing Each Student's Unique Strengths, Passions, and Talents.*

The FLOOR	The Five Shifts	Shift Elements
F	**1. Fallacy of Fixed Intelligence**	**Challenging the misconception of "Smart"** • Understanding how the brain functions in relation to learning. • Understanding brain-based strategies to enhance educational practices. **Growth mindset:** • Embracing a growth mindset as an educator. • Cultivating a growth mindset in students and a belief in their unique genius.
L	**2. Labels Be Gone**	**Understanding the negative effects of marginalizing labels.** • Examining how labels can create fixed mindsets and limit individuals' unlimited potential. • Exploring how labels can shape beliefs, expectations, and actions in educational settings and life and what we can do about it.
O	**3. Obligation of Teams**	**Highlighting the importance of collective teacher efficacy and collective responsibility.** • Encouraging educators to embrace vulnerability and to share their own expertise with each other. • Creating a receptive and supportive environment for growth and learning.
O	**4. Our Superpowers**	**Understanding how habits shape our daily lives and influence our actions.** **Educator superpowers:** • 7 powerful strategies for educators that yield significant educational outcomes. **Student superpowers:** • Highlighting the importance of 7 attributes for student confidence.
R	**5. Resistance & Inspiration**	**Acknowledging and addressing challenges or obstacles that may arise in the educational context.** • Offering strategies to overcome resistance and create a supportive learning environment. **Highlighting examples of inspiration ensures that this is possible and doable.** • School districts and individuals' stories.

CHAPTER 1

F = Fallacy of Fixed Intelligence

"Children grow into the intellectual life around them."

—LEV VYGOTSKY[23]

The Science of Learning and the Brain

"Nobody is born smart. We all start at zero, cannot talk, cannot walk, certainly can't do algebra, add, read, write, riding a bike. Nobody is good at anything at first. There was a time when Einstein could not count to 10, and Shakespeare had to learn his ABCs like the rest of us. Thankfully we are born to learn. Slowly, you stumble, slip, crawl, fall, and fail and fall. Frustrating, confusing, trying, struggling, until one day you walk one foot in front of the other, one idea on top of the next, each wrong answer making your brain stronger. Failing is just another word for growing, and you keep going. Whoever you are, wherever you are, you only must know one thing, you can learn anything."[24]

23. Vygotsky, Lev, *Mind in Society: The Development of Higher Psychological Processes*, Harvard University Press, 1978, pp. 88, 89-90, 86. https://newlearningonline.com/new-learning/chapter-8/reflexivity-towards-new-learning/vygotsky-on-the-zone-of-proximal-development#:~:text=Vygotsky%20explains%20the%20way%20in,life%20of%20those%20around%20them.

24. "You Can Learn Anything," Khan Academy Video, August 19, 2014, https://youtu.be/JC82Il2cjqA.

Students Are Much More Than a Score: 790

As an educator, I have often shared my personal experience as a student who lacked confidence. Reading was challenging, and I constantly needed assistance to improve my fluency. Tests and assignments would trigger panic attacks, especially during elementary school. I often felt I needed to do better. Despite having caring teachers who wanted the best for me, I never felt confident as a learner. I did okay when I could navigate the system to do extra homework. I diligently followed instructions and remained compliant.

One incident that reinforced my belief of not being smart occurred during high school when I took the Scholastic Aptitude Test (SAT). On my first attempt, I scored a combined reading and math total of 790. However, my second attempt resulted in a score of 730. Fortunately, I was an accomplished basketball player and was recruited by Division I schools. George Washington University's cutoff score for any Division I athlete then was 700. Although my grades were average in high school, never surpassing a 2.7 grade point average (GPA) and never making the honor roll, I managed to get into George Washington due to my athletic ability. Once in college, I excelled and completed my undergraduate degree ahead of schedule in three and a half years.

After obtaining my bachelor's degree, I pursued a teaching certification, a master's degree, and certification as an administrator. The rest is history. I have enjoyed an incredible career, but I sometimes think about one incident around my SAT score. During a conversation with classmates about our SAT scores, one student proudly boasted about scoring 1580. When he asked about my score, I hesitated and said I didn't achieve 1580, feeling embarrassed to reveal my actual scores of 790 and 730. At the time, I believed that these scores defined my intelligence. Despite lacking confidence as a learner, even through high school, I had the privilege of having two exceptional teachers, Ms. Ann Stephenson for U.S. History in 11th grade and Ms. Brenda Cox for Physics in 12th grade, who made me feel like the most brilliant student in their classes. From what I know now, they made each student feel that way!

From Misplaced Score to Life's Turning Point: The 1480 Effect

Justin Prince recounted a story on his Instagram page about an individual from Wichita, Kansas, who faced challenges in high school, associating with the wrong crowd and struggling academically. In his junior year, he decided to take the SATs, scoring an unexpectedly high 1480 out of 1600. Despite skepticism, the person's mother questioned whether he had cheated, which he denied. Motivated by the score, he transformed his behavior, left negative influences behind, and excelled in school. This change led him to graduate with honors, attend an Ivy League school, become an entrepreneur in the magazine industry, and achieve substantial success.

However, later in life, a letter revealed he had been sent the wrong score; his actual score was 740, not 1480. Reflecting on this revelation, the person realized that his life had been influenced not by the number itself but by his belief and confidence in that supposed achievement. He expressed, "My whole life changed, and I started acting like 1480."[25] This prompts us to consider what might have transpired if the correct score of 740 had been known from the start. How would his path have differed, and would he have still achieved the remarkable transformation that shaped his life?

Now I understand that we are so much more than a test score. We have evidence that a test score does not define our intelligence. Various factors contribute to test scores. As we delve into the topic of the brain and learning, all your students must remember that when you administer tests or assessments, those scores should not determine their destiny.

How well-versed are you and your colleagues on the brain and the science of learning? Do you truly grasp the unlimited potential that lies within each student? Understanding these foundational aspects is paramount in creating an environment that fosters gifted experiences and unleashes this boundless potential. In this chapter, we will delve

---

25. Prince, Justin, "Flunking Out," https://www.instagram.com/reel/CtjqoXjAzp-F/?igshid=MTc4MmM1YmI2Ng==.

into and explore the remarkable capabilities of the brain and the power it has on learning. By immersing ourselves in this knowledge, we can unlock new possibilities, challenge existing limitations, and empower our students to reach beyond what they ever thought possible.

In the book *Time for Change*, authors Anthony Muhammad and Luis Cruz discuss why people resist change. One of the reasons they say that people resist change is because those responsible for implementation often do not give the rationale for the change. People want to know why they need to change. In a keynote speech, Luis shared, *"People will resist if, first, we're not explaining to people why we must change. Why do we need to change? If you haven't made that clear, if you haven't made it clear that all kids need to learn at high levels, if you have not made it clear that not all kids were born on third base, then your people are left wondering why."*[26]

In the following sections, we will do just this: learn about the brain, some crucial parts and chemicals, and how they work as we know it today. Yes, as we know about the brain and the latest research that we have today. In her thesis, "Empathy, and the Role of Mirror Neurons," Margaret Steward quoted American philosopher John R. Searle: *"Because we do not understand the brain very well, we are constantly tempted to use the latest technology as a model for trying to understand it."*[27]

Neuroscience has accelerated our understanding of the brain and its complexities. However, I'll take a bold guess and say that in thirty years, some of what we know will either be outdated or expanded upon with the advance of new technologies.

In this section, we'll talk about why it's essential to understand how our brain works and how we learn. We'll also learn that having a fixed amount of intelligence from the start isn't true. Our brain can get

---

26. Muhammad, Anthony and Cruz, Luis, *Time For Change: 4 Essential Skills for Transformational School and District Leaders*, Solution Tree Press, 2019.

27. Steward, Margaret, *Empathy and the Role of Mirror Neurons*, Regis University, 2017, https://epublications.regis.edu/cgi/viewcontent.cgi?article=1827&context=theses.

smarter as we learn, stay curious, and keep trying. It's also influenced by what adults think and expect from students.

As we learn together, consider the following quotes:

"Teachers are brain changers. Thus, it would seem obvious that an understanding of the brain—the organ of learning—would be critical to a teacher's readiness to work with students.

Unfortunately, most teachers lack an understanding of how the brain receives, filters, consolidates, and applies learning for both the short and long term."[28]

"Low Socioeconomic Status children (with a mean I.Q. of 77) adopted by high-SES parents averaged I.Q. gains of 21 points when tested eight years later."[29]

"When children understand how their brains change as they learn new things, the whole idea of learning in school could change profoundly for them."[30]

"Neuroscience research has substantiated these theories through MRI and PET scans that illustrate that when the brain is engaged and encounters challenging tasks and 'complex environments' supported by mediated feedback, new neural patterns are established. These neuro patterns give rise to enhanced memory and intellectual behavior, and they enable high levels of performance."[31]

---

28. Whitman, Glenn and Kelleher, Ian, *Neuroteach: Brain Science and the Future of Education*, Rowman & Littlefield, 2016.

29. Duyme M., Dumaret, A. C., and Tomkiewicz, S. (1999), "How can we boost IQs of 'dull children'?: A late adoption study," *Proceedings National Academy of Sciences USA* 96: pp. 8790-8794.

30. "Putting Neuroscience in the Classroom: How the Brain Changes As We Learn," Pew, April 13, 2020, https://www.pewtrusts.org/en/trend/archive/spring-2020/putting-neuroscience-in-the-classroom-how-the-brain-changes-as-we-learn.

31. Jackson, Yvette citing Feuerstein, Reuven, in *The Pedagogy of Confidence Inspiring High Intellectual Performance in Urban Schools*, Teachers College Press, 2011, p. 94.

The Parts of the Brain and Learning

If we help students believe that they have unlimited capacity to learn, it starts here with our learning about the brain and then for educators to teach them about their brains. Remember what I wrote earlier: Giving people access to the same information simultaneously will provide a better likelihood of them coming to the same conclusions.

There are several ways to think about the brain and its components, but for this book, we will focus on a few areas that I have focused on in my work. The basic descriptions of these functions have been over-simplified. The areas that will be covered are **neurons**, the nerve cells that make up the brain; specific structures such as the **brain stem, amygdala, hippocampus, cerebellum, cerebrum, and prefrontal cortex**; and brain chemicals or neurotransmitters, meaning **cortisol, dopamine, oxytocin, serotonin, and epinephrine**. This section aims to help the reader gain some basic shared understanding of the brain regarding learning.

Think of the brain as a hard-working factory, and just like a factory, it has different areas with unique responsibilities. A lot is happening in our heads. The brain is the organ that is protected by the eight cranial bones. There are eight cranial bones and fourteen facial bones that make up the skull.

In looking at an actual brain, it is a grayish-pink color. Our brain weighs about three pounds, roughly the same as a laptop, a weighted blanket, a fire extinguisher, or 1.4 liters of water. That represents about 2 percent of our body weight. The human heart pumps blood to the entire body and pumps about 20 percent of its total blood output to the brain. Our brain is essential, which is why so much blood travels there!

What Are Neurons and Why Are They Important?

The scientific study of the brain and its functions at the *neuron* level is called *neuroscience*.

Suzana Herculano-Houzelon, a neuroscientist and associate professor of psychological science at Vanderbilt University, devised a new way to count brain cells. She said that we have approximately 86 billion nerve cells or neurons. Each transmits electrochemical signals. For comparison, a dog has around two billion.[32] *Neurons* communicate with one another by sending out electrical and chemical signals through a small pocket of space between them called a *synapse*. Next is a very simplified and condensed explanation of this process.

Neurons have branches called dendrites that receive signals from other neurons using chemicals called neurotransmitters. These signals cause changes in the cell's body (soma) and are then sent to the axon. A strong signal in the axon creates an "action potential," which travels down the axon, covered in insulating material. The signal reaches the axon terminals, releasing neurotransmitters to communicate with other neurons. This process repeats to make connections and store information.

Making more neuron connections helps us store information and become smarter. When we're curious, neurons prepare to communicate. Trying new things creates new connections, and learning new skills makes new pathways, making us smarter.

In the article "You Can Grow Your Intelligence," Lisa Blackwell states, "When you lift weights, your muscles get bigger, and you get stronger. A person who cannot lift 20 pounds when they start exercising can get strong enough to lift 100 pounds after working out for a long time. That is because the muscles become larger and stronger with exercise. Furthermore, when a person stops exercising, the muscles shrink and get weaker. That is why people say, 'Use it or lose it.'"[33]

Our capacity to learn is unlimited!

32. Herculano-Houzel, Suzana, "How Many Neurons Are in the Brain?," BrainFacts. org, December 4, 2018, https://www.youtube.com/watch?v=efLp7nqtlgc&t=105s.

33. Blackwell, Lisa, "You can Grow Your Intelligence," Mindset Works, April 2016, https://www.mindsetworks.com/websitemedia/youcangrowyourintelligence.pdf.

OUR BRAIN
The Cerebrum, Cerebellum, and Brain Stem

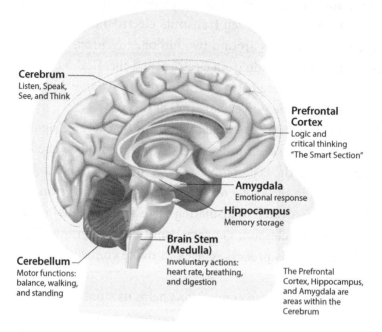

Cerebrum
Listen, Speak, See, and Think

Prefrontal Cortex
Logic and critical thinking
"The Smart Section"

Amygdala
Emotional response

Hippocampus
Memory storage

Brain Stem (Medulla)
Involuntary actions: heart rate, breathing, and digestion

Cerebellum
Motor functions: balance, walking, and standing

The Prefrontal Cortex, Hippocampus, and Amygdala are areas within the Cerebrum

Cerebrum

The cerebrum is the most significant part of our brain, and it plays a vital role in learning and thinking. It consists of two halves called hemispheres, the *right hemisphere* and the *left hemisphere*. A bundle of fibers connects these hemispheres called the *corpus callosum*, allowing them to communicate. The cerebrum has a wrinkled outer layer called the cerebral cortex, which is responsible for many of our higher mental functions.

Prefrontal Cortex

The Prefrontal Cortex is in the front part of the brain in the cerebrum, right behind our forehead. It is responsible for important cognitive functions such as decision-making, problem-solving, and logical thinking. This part of the brain helps us plan our actions, control our emotions, and set goals. It also plays a role in shaping our personality and values.

Important Note:

Mary Fernandez wrote in her article "Brain Development and Car Rentals" that the lack of a fully developed prefrontal cortex and rational decision-making is why rental car companies only rent to people once they reach age 25. Although many studies previously suggest that a person's prefrontal cortex is fully developed when they are around 25, that is now being questioned.[34]

According to Melanie Whyte, citing neuroscience expert Patrick Porter, Ph.D., founder and CEO of Brain Tap, the brain's development doesn't have an end date. While it's true that the prefrontal cortex takes longer to develop, the age 25 is not a hard number—"it's more of a range." What we do know is that the prefrontal cortex develops after the amygdala.[35]

Amygdala

The *amygdala* is a small structure deep inside the brain, within the cerebrum. It is like the brain's emotional center. The Amygdala helps us experience and process emotions such as happiness, fear, anger, and excitement. It plays a significant role in recognizing and responding to different emotional situations.

> When Maya reacts emotionally to challenging situations, she is using her amygdala.

Hippocampus

The *hippocampus* is another structure located deep within the brain, close to the center of the *cerebrum*. It is crucial for memory formation and retrieval. The *hippocampus* helps us store and remember information, events, and experiences. It plays a vital role in learning new things and recalling memories.

34. Fernandez, Mary, "Brain Development and Car Rentals," LinkedIn, 2015, https://www.linkedin.com/pulse/brain-development-rental-cars-mary-fernandez.

35. Whyte, Mary, "Is 19 Too Young to Get Engaged?," PopSugar, April 12, 2023, https://www.popsugar.com/fitness/prefrontal-cortex-development-49102332.

As Maya learns new things and remembers essential information for her school subjects, she's using her hippocampus.

Cerebellum

The cerebellum is a smaller region located at the back of the brain, below the cerebrum. It is often referred to as the *"little brain."* While the cerebrum is responsible for higher cognitive functions, the cerebellum primarily involves coordination, balance, and precise movements. It helps us with walking, running, writing, and playing sports. The cerebellum ensures that our movements are smooth, accurate, and well-coordinated.

When Maya participates in physical activities like writing, playing sports, or even walking around the school, her cerebellum is at work, helping her maintain balance, coordination, and precise movements.

Brain Stem

The *brain stem* is a vital part of the brain that connects directly to the spinal cord. It is located at the base of the brain, below the cerebellum. The brain stem controls many essential functions necessary for survival, such as breathing, heart rate, blood pressure, digestion, and sleep. It also helps regulate crucial bodily functions without consciously thinking about them.

Even when Maya isn't consciously thinking about it, her brain stem works hard to control vital functions like breathing, heart rate, and digestion, ensuring her survival. At the same time, she focuses on her school activities.

Gaining a basic understanding of the different parts of the brain helps us appreciate the complexity of our incredible organ and how it contributes to our thoughts, emotions, memories, movements, and overall functioning. It allows us to truly grasp the intricate nature of this remarkable organ and comprehend how it influences how we learn.

Reinforcing Learning

Use the information from above to identify which parts of the brain would be working together after reading the following three scenarios:

Scenario #1

Which two parts of the brain would you be using if you were talking to your friend and riding a skateboard? Can you identify the two areas that could work together?

Scenario #2

Which two parts of the brain would you be using if you were trying to remember something your friend said while you decided whether you wanted a banana or watermelon for a snack?

Scenario #3

Which two parts of the brain would you use if you were looking at your phone tracking the taxi/rideshare car while feeling stressed that you would be late?

The parts of the brain that we learned about in the previous section are all responsible for essential tasks. With knowledge, understanding, and awareness, you can control how these structures work together. This knowledge will help you help students unlock their unlimited potential. Now let us learn about some vital brain chemicals, otherwise called neurotransmitters.

Brain Chemicals (Neurotransmitters)

CORTISOL, DOPAMINE, OXYTOCIN, SEROTONIN, AND ADRENALINE/ENDORPHINS (EPINEPHRINE)

"The key thing in understanding brain-based learning is to say what we know about the brain already, which can help us tie this to education to help improve student learning. For example, every educator should know how the brain gets attention and how we keep it; we should know what changes the brain and what factors help make kids smarter. What is the connection between your work and how our brain works?"[36]

Cortisol—The Stress Hormone

Stress refers to two things: the psychological perception of pressure, on the one hand, and the body's response to it, on the other, which involves multiple systems, from metabolism to muscles to memory.

Some stress is necessary for all living systems; it is how they encounter and respond to the challenges and uncertainties of existence. The perception of danger sets off an automatic response system, known as the fight-or-flight response, that, activated through hormonal signals, prepares us to meet a threat or flee from it.

According to research from the University of Rochester, children living in low-income households who endure family instability and emotionally distant caregivers are at risk of impaired cognitive abilities. *"Moderate amounts of cortisol is a good thing, though; it helps facilitate cognitive functioning,"* said psychologist Jennifer Suor. *"In the right amount, it makes you rise to the occasion and helps recruit important cognitive resources like memory and the ability to reason. Nevertheless, it is a problem when we have too much or too little Cortisol."*[37]

---

36. Jensen, Eric, "Brain Based Learning," YouTube, November 4, 2011, https://www.youtube.com/watch?v=HyYhoCqo58w.

37. "Stress in low-income families can affect children's learning," News Center, June 18, 2015, https://www.rochester.edu/newscenter/stress-in-low-income-families-can-affect-childrens-learning-108182/.

In his 2015 article, Christopher Bergland highlighted the significance of cortisol levels and family adversities in influencing children's cognitive development from low-income backgrounds. The study suggests that understanding and managing cortisol activity and addressing specific family stressors can be crucial in promoting positive cognitive outcomes for these children. This finding can shape preventive interventions that reduce family stress and foster strong parent-child relationships to support healthy cortisol levels and enhance cognitive functioning in disadvantaged children.[38]

In *I Thought I Was Going Crazy*, Darryl Webster delves into the challenges children face in their academic journey due to adverse factors linked to stress. Stress, acting as a catalyst, releases cortisol, impacting children's well-being and performance. Darryl references the "Adverse Childhood Experiences (ACEs)" study, which involved Kaiser Permanente members responding to a questionnaire about potentially traumatic events from their childhood.[39]

Adverse Childhood Experiences (ACEs) are potentially traumatic events that occur in childhood (0-17 years), such as experiencing violence, abuse, or neglect, witnessing violence in the home, and having a family member attempt or die by suicide. Also included are aspects of the child's environment that can undermine their sense of safety, stability, and bonding, such as growing up in a household with substance misuse, mental health problems, or instability due to parental separation or incarceration of a parent, sibling, or other members of the home. Toxic stress from ACEs can change brain development and affect how the body responds to stress.

"Traumatic events in childhood can be emotionally painful or distressing and can have effects that persist for years. Factors such as the nature, frequency, and seriousness of the traumatic event, prior history

---

38. Bergland, Christopher, "How Do Various Cortisol Levels Impact Cognitive Functioning?" *Psychology Today*, June 17, 2015, https://www.psychologytoday.com/us/blog/the-athletes-way/201506/how-do-various-cortisol-levels-impact-cognitive-functioning.

39. Webster, Darryl, *I Thought I Was Going Crazy: Overcoming Stress, Anxiety, and Depression*, Achievement-Destiny, pp. 130-132.

of trauma, and available family and community support can shape a child's response to trauma."[40]

According to Arkansas Child Development and Early Learning Standards Birth through 60 Months, "children who lack nurturing relationships with adults and have adverse experiences that cause high levels of stress for prolonged periods (known as toxic stress) may have impaired executive functioning or other cognitive delays. Children who live in extreme poverty, lack stable relationships at home, or live with drug or alcohol-dependent caregivers are more susceptible to toxic stress."[41]

Toxic or chronic stress over a long period can devastate the hippocampus, the brain area responsible for storing our memory. Too many ACEs could decrease cortisol regulation in children, affecting attention, perception, short-term memory, learning, and word retrieval.

There are both healthy and unhealthy responses to stress. Unhealthy responses can include turning to alcohol, drugs, or binge eating. Healthy coping strategies include meditation, exercise, journaling, practicing gratitude, and letting go of what is beyond our control.

> **When Keyshawn faces a surprise pop quiz in school, his body releases cortisol, the stress hormone, to help him cope. While a moderate amount of cortisol can sharpen his thinking and memory, too much can make it harder for him to concentrate and learn effectively.**

---

40. "Violence Prevention—Adverse Childhood Experiences," Center for Disease Control and Prevention, https://www.cdc.gov/violenceprevention/aces/index.html.

41. "Arkansas Child Development and Early Learning Standards Birth through 60 months," Arkansas Head Start, 2016, https://www.arheadstart.org/Ark_Early_Learning_Standards%20(19)%20(1).pdf.

The Happy Brain Chemicals/Neurotransmitters

When a person feels good, the brain releases happiness chemicals or hormones. There are four main happiness brain chemicals, which also may affect a person's stress response.

Dopamine: Joy from accomplishing a goal or succeeding at a task

Dopamine plays a crucial role in enabling motivation, learning, and pleasure while significantly influencing a person's mood due to its involvement in the brain's reward system. When something rewarding happens, dopamine floods the synapses between neurons, leading to that exhilarating feeling of joy upon achieving a goal or succeeding at a task. Moreover, dopamine plays a vital role in the brain's response to stress, facilitating adaptation to various environmental stimuli.

Aside from its stress-coping abilities, dopamine has numerous positive effects. It promotes wakefulness and aids the pancreas in releasing the appropriate amount of insulin after eating. Additionally, dopamine coordinates the brain and body, facilitating voluntary movements such as writing, typing, and driving a car.

> When Keyshawn accomplishes a task or achieves a goal at school, dopamine is released in his brain, making him feel joyful and motivated. This neurotransmitter also helps him adapt to different situations, improving his learning experience.

Oxytocin: The trust and relationship hormone

Oxytocin is a powerful neurotransmitter that fosters feelings of trust and motivates individuals to build and maintain relationships. It is released by the brain's hypothalamus through the pituitary gland, triggering responses throughout the body. By forming strong connections based on loyalty and trust, oxytocin enables individuals to create meaningful relationships with friends and family. The next time you interact with loved ones, take a moment to appreciate the impact of this chemical messenger, as your body relies on oxytocin for both physical and social well-being, contributing to a fulfilling life filled with love and connection.

> When Keyshawn interacts positively with his teachers at school, oxytocin is released in his brain, fostering trust and a stronger bond. This neurotransmitter helps him build meaningful relationships with the staff in the school, contributing to his emotional well-being and enhancing his learning experience through connection and support.

Serotonin: The mood and sleep regulator

Serotonin significantly influences mood, promoting feelings of well-being and happiness. Additionally, serotonin helps achieve restful sleep and regulate the body's internal clock. When there is an imbalance in serotonin levels, individuals may experience a lower mood and difficulties with sleep, leading to confusion and brain fog.

Serotonin's impact is not limited to the brain; it also operates in the small intestine, promoting feelings of satisfaction after eating and regulating appetite. Furthermore, serotonin helps the body identify and eliminate potentially harmful or spoiled foods, triggering feelings of nausea as a protective mechanism. It serves as a warning signal to dispose of toxic substances consumed quickly.

> When Keyshawn experiences positive social interactions and feels confident in his abilities at school, serotonin is released in his brain, promoting feelings of well-being and happiness. This neurotransmitter also contributes to his quality of sleep and helps regulate his internal body clock, aiding in his focus and clarity during classes. As he maintains a balanced serotonin level, Keyshawn benefits not only in mood and sleep but also in his digestion and overall sense of satisfaction.

Adrenaline/Endorphins (Epinephrine): The fight or flight response

Adrenaline, or epinephrine, allows individuals to experience brief euphoria to mask physical pain. It is released in large amounts, leading to various effects on the body, including increased heart rate and blood pressure. This neurotransmitter is responsible for the body's fight-or-flight response.

Adrenaline is a defense mechanism against stress, enabling the body to react swiftly in critical situations. For example, when running late and fearing missing an appointment, epinephrine accelerates breathing and heart rate, facilitating a quick dash to the destination. Additionally, adrenaline sharpens decision-making abilities, such as during tests. However, excessive adrenaline can lead to anxiety, irritability, and difficulty sleeping. Understanding how neurotransmitters like adrenaline function is crucial for managing stress and promoting overall well-being.[42]

> As Keyshawn faces challenging situations at school, like test-taking or rushing to his next class, his body releases adrenaline, which increases his heart rate and sharpens his decision-making. This neurotransmitter helps him react swiftly and stay focused, but too much of it can lead to feelings of anxiety and trouble sleeping. Knowing how adrenaline works is essential for Keyshawn to manage stress and maintain his well-being in his school life.

As our knowledge about the changes in the developing brain during learning increases, our ability to support young learners improves.

Now That You Know

Please take a moment to answer the following questions to reinforce your learning about brain chemicals/neurotransmitters.

1. What is the stress hormone? What effects can chronic stress have on students?

---

42. "7 Neurotransmitters Involved in the Brain-Body Connection," Ask the Scientists, https://askthescientists.com/neurotransmitters/#toggle-id-1.

2. Building trusting relationships with students activates which neurotransmitter? Why is it important to know this information?

3. An imbalance in this neurotransmitter affects mood and sleep. Why is this important to know for students?

4. Accomplishing a goal or task activated which neurotransmitter? How could this be important for students?

5. This brain chemical is the main defense against stress and increases the heart rate and blood pressure:

6. Give an example of how the release of this neurotransmitter could help a student in a stressful situation.

The ACEs study was referenced earlier in this chapter, and these adverse childhood experiences impact the brain chemicals and, ultimately, students' daily and future lives. The study listed ten possible ACEs and concluded that students with four or more ACEs risk long-term impacts on their lives (like ill health and depression), are more likely to drop out of school, and earn far less than those with less than four ACEs throughout their lives.

I have heard educators honestly say: We did not create these situations for students, so what do you want us to do? I understand the overwhelming nature of students coming to us with many challenges. However, if we believe that we are "in loco parentis"—in other words, we are educators in place of a parent—in that case, it is our moral obligation and responsibility to do for them what we would do for our children.

Having laid the foundation of understanding essential brain parts and chemicals concerning learning, we focus on actionable strategies to support your students effectively. As educators, we acknowledge the diverse challenges students may face. Still, it's our moral duty to step into the role of nurturing each student's unique strengths, passions, and talents, especially when they are in our care at school.

Instead of dwelling on the obstacles we didn't create, we will use those obstacles as context and plan accordingly. Let's redirect our attention to the question: What new tools can we acquire and utilize to help every student succeed today?

In this pursuit, we highlight three powerful avenues that stand out at the end of this chapter, each of which can yield significant benefits without requiring a substantial financial investment. These avenues are movement and exercise, relationships, and fostering a growth mindset. Exploring and implementing these strategies in our schools can significantly impact our students' learning and development.

Movement and Exercise: Understanding the role of physical activity in enhancing cognition and promoting learning is crucial. Simple practices like incorporating movement breaks in classrooms and encouraging physical activities can significantly boost students' attention, focus, and overall well-being.

Relationships: Building strong connections with students fosters a positive and supportive learning environment. When students feel valued, understood, and cared for, they are likelier to engage in learning and unlock their unlimited potential.

Growth Mindset: Encouraging a growth mindset in students can transform their approach to challenges and failures. By teaching them that intelligence and abilities can be developed through effort and perseverance, we empower them to embrace learning opportunities and overcome obstacles.

The power of these approaches lies in their accessibility and immediate applicability. As educators, we have the power to implement these strategies right away without the need for significant financial resources. By doing so, we can create an enriching educational experience that caters to the diverse needs of our students and maximizes their potential for success.

Movement, Exercise, and the Brain

Movement and exercise are essential to support the healthy development of students' brains. It involves incorporating physical activity and regular exercise into their daily routines to promote overall well-being. As teachers, we can prioritize movement and exercise by integrating activities that involve movement into our lessons, providing opportunities for physical activity during breaks and advocating for physical education and active lifestyles. By emphasizing the importance of movement and exercise, we help students develop healthy habits, enhance their cognitive function, manage stress, and improve their overall physical and mental well-being.

A Simple Strategy to Improve Students' Brains—MOVE!

Did you know that incorporating exercise into your students' daily routine can benefit their brains? Researcher Wendy Suzuki shared fascinating insights about the positive effects of exercise on the brain, mood, and cognitive function. By implementing exercise strategies in the learning environment, you can create a supportive atmosphere that promotes optimal learning and well-being.[43]

Exercise has immediate effects on the brain. A single workout session increases neurotransmitters like dopamine and serotonin, boosting mood and making students happier. It also improves their ability to focus and pay attention, significantly enhancing their learning experience. Encouraging short movement breaks or physical activities throughout the day can keep their brains alert and engaged.

Additionally, exercise has long-lasting effects on the brain's structure and function. Regular physical activity stimulates the growth of new brain cells in the hippocampus, a region vital for memory formation. Regularly exercising, students can improve their long-term memory and retain information more effectively. It also strengthens the prefrontal cortex, the area responsible for decision-making and attention, improving cognitive abilities.

Exercise plays a protective role in brain health. Students can build solid and resilient brains by promoting an active lifestyle. This

---

43. Ted, "Suzuki, Wendy: The brain-changing benefits of exercise," YouTube, March 21, 2018, https://www.youtube.com/watch?v=BHY0FxzoKZE.

can help prevent neurodegenerative diseases like Alzheimer's and dementia in the future. Encouraging students to embrace physical activity inside and outside the classroom promotes their long-term brain health.

Incorporating exercise doesn't have to be complicated or time-consuming. Simple activities like stretching, dancing, or taking short walks can make a significant difference. Consider integrating movement breaks, active learning strategies, or physical education exercises into your teaching practices. By prioritizing exercise, you support your student's physical well-being and enhance their cognitive abilities and overall academic performance.

Educators can harness the power of exercise to create an optimal learning environment for our students. Promoting physical activity and its many benefits can help them thrive academically, emotionally, and neurologically. We can inspire students to move, learn, and grow their amazing brains!

In our earlier learning about the brain and neurotransmitters, we learned about serotonin, dopamine, and norepinephrine (or adrenaline). Did you know that exercise improves and helps regulate these chemical levels? This, in turn, contributes to our mental alertness and overall well-being. Katie Koeppel shared how she and her teammates successfully incorporated movement into their classrooms. Let's take a closer look at what she had to say.

"Classroom Movement and Brain Breaks: Energize, Engage, Excel!"

AS TOLD BY KATIE KOEPPEL, FORMER THIRD GRADE TEACHER

As an educator, I find it most comfortable to rely on visuals and audio when teaching our students. Lessons can easily be adapted with pictures, icons, or recordings to cater to their learning styles. However, incorporating movement into lessons requires stepping out of my comfort zone and actively engaging with the content. At first, it might have felt uncomfortable and unnatural, but I have realized that adding movement in the classroom tremendously impacts our students' learning experiences.

To infuse movement into our classrooms, my team and I explored various creative approaches, and one successful method was through music. We would play science songs, and the students would eagerly sing and dance along to the lyrics. As a class, we would create specific movements for different parts of the song, making the learning process fun and interactive. For instance, if our learning target was identifying producers, consumers, and decomposers, we acted out these roles while the Decomposer's song played.

This combination of music and movement truly engaged our students. It breathed life into the academic content, and I noticed that it helped combat academic fatigue. The connection between music and academics allowed students to absorb the information more enthusiastically. When they had a movement or song to tie their learning to, they retained vocabulary and knowledge for extended periods, indicating a deeper understanding of the subject matter.

What's most fulfilling about incorporating movement in the classroom is that it gives all students access to the lesson. Regardless of labels based on language acquisition or educational levels, every student is given an entry point to participate and engage actively. The movements are modeled and reinforced, fostering a safe and exciting learning environment. Students feel encouraged to participate, boosting their confidence and success in applying their knowledge.

Despite the numerous benefits of movement-based learning,

some teachers may oppose the idea for various reasons. It requires us to move away from the traditional teaching method of having students sit at their desks for extended periods. Incorporating movement requires purposeful planning, clear expectations, and establishing boundaries to ensure a productive learning experience.

In addition to incorporating movement, my team and I recognized the importance of brain breaks in the classroom. These quick breaks allow students to pause from their academic tasks and engage in relaxation or movement activities. As classroom teachers, we found brain breaks essential for improving student focus and concentration, reducing academic fatigue, and enhancing the overall well-being of our classroom community.

Whether it's a dance session or Kids' yoga, brain breaks offer a valuable opportunity for students to recharge during their academically rigorous day. I've observed that at the end of a long instructional block, students can appear low-energy and fatigued. Engaging them in a game or dance rejuvenates their energy, increasing alertness and focus for the next lesson.

Incorporating brain breaks doesn't have to be a time-consuming process. With a toolbox of brain breaks readily available, my team and I pulled from various activities whenever necessary. We understand that some teachers may worry about losing instructional time, but taking the time for brain breaks results in greater student alertness and overall productivity. Brain breaks can be as short as a few minutes and easily incorporated into morning meetings and transitions, minimizing disruptions in core academic areas.

Moreover, brain breaks create a welcoming class environment and foster a sense of social connectedness among students. Students feel safe in their learning environment and are more likely to take risks and actively participate in challenging academic tasks. As teachers participate in brain breaks alongside their students, we lead by example and strengthen our students' sense of classroom community. These positive interactions during brain breaks extend to other academic and behavioral aspects of our student's lives.

Through the incorporation of movement and brain breaks, my team and I witnessed a positive impact on our students' learning experiences. Embracing these strategies enabled us to create a learning environment that fosters growth, engagement, and overall well-being.[44]

The insights from Katie Koeppel's "Classroom Movement and Brain Breaks" emphasize the importance of brain-based learning strategies benefiting all students, particularly those who may grapple with consistent trauma. As we work toward making gifted education a FLOOR for every student, we must acknowledge how trauma can impact academic growth. By adopting techniques that activate the cerebellum and stimulate the release of the "happy brain neurotransmitters," we can help all students engage, creating a level playing field. Through these strategies, we foster an inclusive and equitable educational environment that supports the success of all students.

Thought Sparks Questions:

1. How do you incorporate movement or physical activities in your classroom? Are there any challenges or barriers you face in implementing such practices?

2. Reflect on a specific lesson or topic that could be enhanced by incorporating movement. How might you integrate movement into that lesson to make it more engaging and memorable for your students?

---

44. Koeppel, Katie, "Classroom Movement and Brain Breaks: Energize, Engage, Excel," personal communication (email), July 23, 2023.

3. Have you noticed any signs of academic fatigue or disengagement among your students during long instructional blocks? How might incorporating brain breaks help address these challenges?

4. What strategies can you implement to ensure that all students, regardless of their learning preferences or abilities, can access movement-based activities and brain breaks in your classroom?

5. How can you overcome resistance or concerns from fellow educators or administrators who may view movement-based learning as a departure from traditional teaching methods? What evidence or research can you present to support the benefits of incorporating movement in the classroom?

Let's Talk About Relationships and the Brain!

As we explored earlier, oxytocin is pivotal in fostering trust and relationships, evident in overall success within organizations and vital teacher-student connections. Across my career, from sports teams to schools and districts, triumphs have hinged on transparent, caring relationships among participants. Significantly, this extends to teacher-student dynamics, where oxytocin plays a crucial role in building trust and enhancing the learning journey.

Consider how institutions with similar plans can yield differing results; the answer lies in the intricate web of interpersonal relationships. In your professional experience, where values like trust, kindness, and recognition are emphasized, do you feel oxytocin's influence motivates you daily? Reflect on how this impacts your rapport with colleagues and students and how nurturing these connections can elevate overall success and well-being.

"Humble leaders who are compassionate, generous, forgiving, and ethical do better. They lead with kindness and keep their employees' well-being in mind."[45]

What you want from your work experiences and the leaders in your school or district is like what students desire. The difference is that they often do not have the maturity, wisdom, or life experiences or have not been taught the skills to articulate what they need.

I have over 35 years of experience as an educator and know our profession is full of kind and compassionate individuals. We can always learn from our colleagues regarding different strategies to build and sustain deep and meaningful relationships with each other and, more importantly, the students whom we serve.

In my former school, Mason Crest Elementary School, we had a behavior team that guided the school in different areas, especially around schoolwide behaviors, proactive approaches, and strategies to support teachers and students. The team would share resources and tools in a regular newsletter emailed to all staff. The following excerpt is about relationships.

Mason Crest Behavior Team Tips for Staff

> Meaningful relationships between teachers and students can be the most critical factor in motivating students to listen, learn and comply with classroom/school expectations. In their work with Love and Logic, Jim Fay and David Funk…found that students who do not feel they enjoy positive relationships with their teachers are more disruptive, are less likely to be academically engaged, and are more likely to drop out.[46] When our students genuinely believe we care about them, they will care about us.

45. Seppälä, Emma and McNichols, Nicole K., "The Power of Healthy Relationships at Work," *Harvard Business Review*, June 21, 2022, https://hbr.org/2022/06/the-power-of-healthy-relationships-at-work.

46. Fay, Jim and Funk, David. *Teaching with Love & Logic: Taking Control of the Classroom*, Love and Logic Press, 1995.

Establishing caring relationships with our students can be done in so many ways and doesn't require above and beyond effort. Noticing new shoes, a new haircut, or taking time to kneel at a student's desk and listen to what they did over the weekend will go far in laying the foundation of a relationship. During lessons, thumbs-up smiles and eye contact can also go far in reminding children that you care about them as more than learners.

We can borrow a few ideas from our colleagues from the first grade and kindergarten teams. The first-grade teachers have lunch bunches with different students from their classes every Monday to help get to know more about their students as individuals and build connections with them outside of academics. The kindergarten teachers have been employing a strategy of "banking time" with some of those students who have presented behavioral challenges, allowing those students to spend time alone with their teachers in the classroom before the other children enter the room to further the students' attachment to their teacher and their classroom.

If you are looking for different ways to connect with students, the behavior team offers a few opportunities that we can take advantage of. Our school's Mentoring Program pairs teacher volunteers with students who need additional attention so that they can enjoy lunch together on a weekly basis. The Paw Pals program pairs teachers with four students whom they touch base with daily to check in for a "hello" and a high five.

These are just a few ideas for building and strengthening relationships between teachers and students. We know there are many other beautiful things that you are doing to improve relationships with students, and we would love it if you would share those with us so that we can feature more ideas in a future weekly behavior tip on relationship building.

HAVE A WONDERFUL WEEK!
YOUR MASON CREST BEHAVIOR TEAM[47]

If our goal is to have students in the right frame of mind to learn and make responsible decisions, it must begin with building positive teacher-student relationships. We will go deeper into student-teacher relationships in Chapter 4; however, setting the table for what is next is essential. Students must be in a safe environment with the right relationships to accept the concept of a growth mindset. Teachers must also embrace and change our mindsets for improvement and learning, which will take trust, vulnerability, and compassion.

Is Our Mind Ready?
Through an Attitude of Continuous Improvement

As we begin this section, consider the following quotes:

> *"I think educators commonly hold two beliefs that do just that. Many believe that (1) praising students' intelligence builds their confidence and motivation to learn, and (2) students' inherent intelligence is the major cause of their achievement in school. Our research has shown that the first belief is false and that the second can be harmful—even for the most competent students."*
>
> —CAROL DWECK[48]

> *"Judging people by their current abilities masks their future potential. Progress depends less on talent than motivation and opportunity. Growth is not about the natural gifts you have—it's about the character you build."*[49]
>
> —ADAM GRANT, 2023, HIDDEN POTENTIAL

47. "Mason Crest Behavior Team Tips for Staff," Mason Crest Elementary School Behavior Team, personal communication, 2012.

48. Dweck, Carol, "The Perils and Promise of Praise," ASCD, October 1, 2007, https://www.ascd.org/el/articles/the-perils-and-promises-of-praise.

49. Grant, Adam, Hidden Potential, Viking, 2023.

In the groundbreaking book *Mindset: The New Psychology of Success*, Carol Dweck coined and defined the terms *fixed mindset* and *growth mindset*.[50] In research studies early in her career, she noted the following as a real turning point:

"I wanted to see how children coped with challenge and difficulty. I gave 10-year-olds problems that were slightly too hard for them. Some of them reacted in a shockingly positive way. They said things like I love a challenge, or, you know, I was hoping this would be informative. They understood that their abilities could be developed. They had what I call a growth mindset.

"However, other students felt it was tragic and catastrophic from their more fixed mindset perspective. Their intelligence had been up for judgment, and they failed. Instead of luxuriating in the power of yet, they were gripped in the tyranny of now. So, what do they do next? I will tell you what they do next. In one study, they told us they would cheat the next time instead of studying more if they failed the test. In another study, after a failure, they looked for someone who did worse than they did so they could feel really good about themselves."

Dweck defined the actions/behaviors as *growth* and *fixed* mindsets. "In a growth mindset, people believe that their most basic abilities can be developed through dedication and hard work—brains and talent are just the starting point. This view creates a love of learning and resilience essential for great accomplishment." In a fixed mindset, people believe their basic qualities, like intelligence or talent, are fixed traits. They spend their time documenting their intelligence or talent instead of developing them. They also believe that talent alone creates success—without effort."[51]

People can have fixed or growth mindsets in academic areas, sports, music, or any endeavor. Growth mindsets and fixed mindsets are beliefs. Moreover, like other beliefs, these can shape our identity and behavior.

---

50. Dweck, Carol, *Mindset: The New Psychology of Success*, Ballantine, 2006.

51. Dweck, Carol, "Carol Dweck Revisits the 'Growth Mindset,'" *Education Week*, September 22, 2015. https://www.edweek.org/leadership/opinion-carol-dweck-revisits-the-growth-mindset/2015/09 on August 1, 2023.

I used to say to myself that I was not good at reading. Some people say they "are not a math person." Some people will say they are "not good athletes or not good at sports." People with a growth mindset are not fatalistic and focus on the process of getting better. People with a growth mindset believe that:

> I am not a good reader YET!

> I am not a math person YET!

> I am not a strong swimmer YET!

The thing about mindset is that one can have a growth mindset in one area (*I am getting better as a tennis player*) and a fixed mindset in another area (*I cannot pass the driver's test because I cannot parallel park*). Making mistakes and being willing to learn from mistakes is part of having a growth mindset. Sometimes, a fixed mindset may be good to protect oneself from harm or perceived danger, such as, *I am never going to cliff dive from a hundred feet.* If one is not a diver and does not like heights, the fixed mindset, in this instance, may be preferable to taking an unnecessary risk. However, when it comes to learning or improving in almost every area of life, a growth mindset will help individuals move positively toward their goals.

As educators, it is essential to help students understand that their mindsets will affect their attitudes toward learning. Students with a fixed mindset think that their intelligence cannot be developed. They avoid challenges, give up easily, see feedback as an attack on them, and feel threatened by the success of others. Holding onto a fixed mindset may result in people achieving less and not realizing their unlimited potential.

Conversely, students with a growth mindset see that their intelligence or abilities can be developed. They embrace challenges, persist in the face of failure, see effort as a way forward toward mastery, embrace and learn from feedback, and look for others who are successful and find inspiration in their wins. Embracing and developing a growth mindset will help people achieve higher levels in school and life.

In their book *Building Blocks for Social-Emotional Learning*, Tracey Hulen and Ann-Bailey Lipsett write about mindset: "We have many thoughts and beliefs, but when those beliefs become patterns of habitual thoughts, they begin to form mental attitudes."[52] In many circles, this is mindfulness or awareness of what we tell ourselves about ourselves or internal self-talk. If we do it repeatedly, and it becomes a pattern, then we tend to act in the way that our mind has been conditioned. It becomes a self-fulfilling prophecy.

Many successful people have failed multiple times before succeeding. Think about yourself and where you are today. Did you arrive here because everything was easy, or are you here because you struggled, had setbacks, got back up, and continued working toward the goal while embracing the journey? What was your mindset?

There are people throughout history who have struggled, and that struggle was why they became successful. Do an internet search of the following people with the keyword phrase "failed before succeeding." I did so recently and got these results.

- Lucille Ball
- Oprah Winfrey
- Vera Wang
- Michael Jordan
- Stephanie Meyer
- J. K. Rowling
- Walt Disney
- Abraham Lincoln
- Thomas Edison
- Venus and Serena Williams

What do these people have in common? What was their mindset? Do you have any idea of what their IQs are/were? Who in your life

---

52. Hulen, Tracey and Lipsett, Ann-Bailey, *Building Blocks for Social-Emotional Learning*, Solution Tree Press, 2022, p. 83.

may not be famous that you can point to regarding failing many times before succeeding?

Handling Hard Better: Kara Lawson, Head Women's Coach, Duke University Basketball

Kara Lawson delivered a speech in 2022 emphasizing the misconception that life will eventually become easier. She shared examples of how people often wait for things to get easier, whether it's getting through a difficult phase or expecting future challenges to be less daunting. However, she challenged this notion by explaining that life never gets easier; individuals become better at handling difficult situations. This mental shift is crucial because it will never happen if we keep waiting for life to become easier. We might find ourselves thinking it's too hard or easier for others, but the truth is that life is hard for everyone.

Lawson highlighted that as we become more adept at handling hardships, we should expect life to throw even more challenges. This is true not just in basketball, academics, or any specific endeavor but in life. Graduating college or achieving certain milestones doesn't mean life suddenly becomes easy; it often becomes even more demanding. Therefore, she encouraged her players to focus on becoming individuals who can handle difficult situations effectively rather than waiting for the easy way out.

Lawson emphasized that any meaningful pursuit, whether winning championships, raising a family, or pursuing personal goals, requires handling hard situations well. Those who can effectively navigate challenges are the ones who achieve their desired outcomes. On the other hand, those who wait for easy solutions are akin to people waiting for a bus that will never arrive.

Lawson advised against waiting for life to become easy. Instead, she encouraged everyone to embrace the difficulty, not get discouraged, and develop the ability to handle hard situations. By doing so, individuals will be well-equipped to face whatever comes their way and achieve greatness.[53]

How effective are we, as educators, instilling in students the ability to embrace challenges and empowering them to navigate difficult circumstances?

Consider and reflect on Kara Lawson's message and the following quotes before proceeding to the next section. (You can see her video by searching "Handle Hard Better" on YouTube.)

> *"It is impossible to live without failing at something unless you live so cautiously that you might as well not have lived at all, in which case you fail by default."*
>
> —J. K. ROWLING[54]

> *"It doesn't matter how far you might rise. At some point, you are bound to stumble. If you're constantly pushing yourself higher and higher, the law of averages predicts that you will, at some point, fall. And when you do, I want you to remember this: There is no such thing as failure. Failure is just life trying to move us in another direction."*
>
> —OPRAH WINFREY[55]

> *"If you're not making mistakes, then you're not doing anything. I'm positive that a doer makes mistakes."*
>
> —JOHN WOODEN[56]

---

53. Duke Women's Basketball, "Handle Hard Better," YouTube, https://www.youtube.com/watch?v=oDzfZOfNki4&t=25s

54. Harvard Magazine, "J.K. Rowling Speaks at Harvard Commencement," YouTube, https://www.youtube.com/watch?v=wHGqp8lz36c&t=7s.

55. "Winfrey's Commencement Address," *The Harvard Gazette*, https://news.harvard.edu/gazette/story/2013/05/winfreys-commencement-address/

56. "About Coach John Wooden," The Wooden Effect, https://www.thewoodeneffect.com/about-coach/.

> *"While one person hesitates because he feels inferior, the other is busy making mistakes, learning from them, and becoming superior."*
>
> —JOHN C. MAXWELL[57]

> *"There's no failure in sports. You know, there's good days, bad days. Some days you are able to be successful. Some days you are not. Some days it's your turn, some days it's not your turn. And that's what sports is about. You don't always win."*
>
> —GIANNIS ANTETOKOUNMPO[58]

Reflections on Kara Lawson's speech and the above quotes:

- What stood out?

- Can you relate? How so?

- Was there ever a time when you gave up? (Hint: We all have.) Why?

- How did you feel?

- Knowing what you know now about brain chemicals, which one(s) were most likely more active as you were deciding to give up and after you gave up?

- Name a time when you persevered in the face of significant obstacles. How did you feel?

- The growth mindset is not just a bunch of strategies; it's a way of thinking. Explain how you focused on getting through that significant obstacle/challenge.

---

57. Maxwell, John, *Leadership Gold: Lessons I've Learned from a Lifetime of Leading,* Thomas Nelson, 2008.

58. Brockington, Ariana, "There's No Failure In Sports," *Today,* April 27, 2023, https://www.today.com/news/sports/giannis-antetokounmpo-responds-failure-question-bucks-loss-rcna81895.

Learning About Mindset as a School Community?
HERE IS ONE APPROACH

At Mason Crest, our goal was to teach students about the power of having a growth mindset. However, how could we effectively do that if we, as educators, still held onto fixed mindsets in certain areas? We took an unconventional step to gain support from the community to foster a shared understanding of our new approach to learning. We invited parents to join us in our learning journey, recognizing their valuable role in shaping their children's education.

We believed parents could be our greatest allies in shifting the narrative around gifted education. So, we invited them to join us during our professional learning sessions. By learning about the brain and the concept of growth versus fixed mindsets, parents could become advocates for our philosophy and share their knowledge with others.

We provided each staff member and participating parent with a book copy to ensure everyone had access to the same information. Some of our teacher leaders took the initiative to create a series of four professional learning sessions based on the book.

Engaging in this collective learning experience was truly transformative for us. It shifted our mindset from thinking, "We cannot get all students to learn at high levels," to recognizing that we had not achieved it yet. It fostered a culture of possibilities, optimism, and a belief that we could make a difference.

Through these sessions, we explored various concepts and ideas, helping us understand that we could guide students in taking ownership of their learning. We encouraged everyone to share their thoughts, observations, and questions. Instead of shutting down ideas with "yeah, but," we challenged ourselves to ask "what if," and consider the possibilities of embracing this deep learning with parents.

We recognized that by collaborating with parents, we could support each other and help even more students succeed. The possibilities of this partnership were inspiring, and we were eager to see the impact it would have on our students' growth and development.

In Their Own Words

Monica Buckhorn, Sandra Miracle, and Richard Rockenbach were three parents who were instrumental in helping to open Mason Crest Elementary School in 2012. These three parents participated in the book study learning sessions around the growth mindset philosophy. Here is what they said in their own words:

Monica Buckhorn

When I was invited to join the learning sessions with the Mason Crest staff about mindset, I had mixed thoughts and reactions. At first, I felt intimidated because I had never heard of a growth mindset before, and I wasn't sure what I was getting myself into. However, I also felt incredibly honored to be a part of the school's learning community. It was evident from the start that Mason Crest was a different kind of school that genuinely cared about building strong relationships with the students, the parents, and the community. As I listened to the staff passionately talk about their approach to teaching and how a growth mindset was at the foundation of their work, I became truly inspired. I knew that this philosophy had the potential to make a positive impact not only on my children but also on every aspect of my life.

My understanding of the growth mindset evolved and deepened throughout the learning journey. Initially, I saw it as a cool idea and a helpful tool to support my children's education. However, I soon realized that a growth mindset was more than just a concept or a tool—it became a guiding philosophy I applied to every aspect of my life. Ten years have passed since then, and I can confidently say that a growth mindset still drives my thinking and shapes my approach to challenges and opportunities.

Participating in the learning sessions had a significant impact on my mindset. It transformed the way I parent and support my children's education. Embracing a growth mindset has allowed me to stay positive and supportive as my children navigate their challenges, whether in school, sports, or life. I've learned to be more empathetic and less reactive when my children face difficulties. Instead of getting frustrated or angry, I focus on asking questions, understanding what strategies work for them, and emphasizing their efforts and progress. A growth mindset has also taught me how to advocate for my children better. I can engage with their teachers and coaches in a way that supports everyone involved while staying true to my children's needs.

During the learning sessions, some concepts resonated with me as a parent. One was the idea of focusing on the "effort" grade rather than solely the "standard" grade. Before the sessions, I had always believed that if my children worked hard, they would automatically achieve good grades. However, I realized that the journey to success is not always linear, and it's essential to recognize and appreciate the effort put in, even when immediate results may not be apparent. Another concept that stood out was the power of the word "yet." It became a go-to word in my vocabulary, reminding me and my children that even if something is challenging now, it doesn't mean it will always be that way. The word "yet" embodies the belief that growth and progress are possible with time, effort, and support.

Incorporating the principles of a growth mindset into my interactions with my children at home became my priority. I shared what I was learning with my family throughout the learning sessions. One of the first changes I made was to emphasize the importance of the effort grade to my children. I assured them that if they put in a strong effort, I wasn't worried about their other grades because I knew they would eventually succeed with the support they received at Mason Crest.

As an active member of the PTO and a proud ambassador for the school, I eagerly discussed growth mindset with other

Mason Crest parents and community members. However, I realized that not everyone fully grasped the power and impact of a growth mindset. Many parents saw it as a good concept but may not have understood its potential to shape their children's lives. I shared information about the growth mindset to bridge this gap and modeled it in my conversations and interactions with parents. Leading by example and embodying growth mindset principles was often more effective than simply telling others about it.

Applying the principles of a growth mindset in my children's education also presented some challenges. It meant letting go of learned behaviors and language and relinquishing some control. Supporting a growth mindset requires allowing children to struggle and fail, knowing there is power and growth in those experiences. Letting go of the urge to intervene and provide immediate solutions constantly has been a continuous learning process for me. However, I remind myself to approach situations in a supportive and positive manner, even when difficult.

A strong partnership between parents and the Mason Crest staff could further enhance the implementation of a growth mindset in the school and other schools my children would attend. When a school authentically embraces a big idea like a growth mindset, educating and engaging parents and the community becomes crucial. As a parent who has always been involved in my children's learning process, I recognized that everyone has a learning curve. Moreover, different cultural norms and family dynamics shape how parents engage with their children's academics. By getting parents to understand and embrace a growth mindset, they can hold themselves accountable and extend that support to other family members, coaches, and adults who influence their child's development.

The knowledge and insights gained from the Mason Crest learning sessions have profoundly impacted my children's academic and personal growth. I have witnessed firsthand the difference a teacher or coach can make in my child's success and self-perception. How educators communicate, particularly when a student is struggling, plays a significant role in how my children react and respond. Teachers who foster a growth mindset and appreciate the effort put into their classes have empowered my children to excel and believe in their abilities.

Now that I have become a classroom teacher I have since embarked on a personal quest to deepen my understanding of the growth mindset. This journey has led me to explore topics such as equity in the classroom and how to authentically provide each student with the support they need to succeed. Embracing a growth mindset goes hand in hand with creating an inclusive and supportive learning environment for all students.[59]

Sandra Miracle

When I was invited to join the learning sessions with the Mason Crest staff to discuss the book *Mindset*, I was truly grateful for the opportunity. It gave me the push I needed to prioritize reading the book, something I had intended to do but had kept putting off due to the busyness of life with three small children. The invitation made me feel valued as a parent, and I realized how important it was to actively participate in this learning journey.

Throughout the learning journey, my understanding of the growth mindset underwent a profound shift. I learned to reframe challenges as opportunities for growth, rather than seeing them as threats or weaknesses. This change in perspective empowered me to tackle challenges with excitement

---

59. Buckhorn, Monica, *Mindset* response, personal communication, June 24, 2023.

and dedication, and I carried this mindset into my parenting approach. I began to focus on my children's consistency and dedication to learning new skills, applauding their efforts and fostering a culture of patience and curiosity in our home.

One concept that resonated deeply with me as a parent was learning how to recognize my own fixed mindset tendencies and develop strategies to foster a more persistent growth mindset. Understanding my natural reactions to failures and setbacks helped me respond to my children's struggles with a more positive and growth-oriented approach. Instead of downplaying or overreacting, I saw their challenges as learning opportunities.

Incorporating the principles of growth mindset into my interactions with my children at home became a priority. I was particularly interested in the information about parental responses to failures and setbacks. Learning to see these moments as opportunities for growth and learning, rather than roadblocks, significantly impacted my approach to parenting. It encouraged my children to keep trying and persist through difficulties, rather than giving up easily.

The knowledge and insights gained from these learning sessions have had a positive impact on both my children's academic and personal growth. By learning in an environment that celebrates the success of others, my children have become better schoolmates and teammates with their peers. They are also encouraged to learn from their mistakes through honest self-reflection, fostering personal growth and development.

Participating in the learning sessions with the Mason Crest staff was a transformative experience for me. It not only deepened my understanding of a growth mindset but also allowed me to apply these principles to my parenting approach. Engaging in this collective learning experience with parents and educators fostered a culture of possibilities and optimism, creating a community that supports and uplifts each other on our growth mindset journey. The impact of this partnership between parents and educators goes beyond the school walls, positively influencing our children's academic achievements and personal development in a profound way.[60]

Richard "Rock" Rockenbach

Being invited to join the learning sessions with the Mason Crest staff about mindset was a delightful surprise for me. As a parent, I have often felt disconnected from the educational process, with limited opportunities for meaningful involvement. However, this initiative by Mason Crest Elementary School offered a refreshing change—an opportunity for parents to actively participate in the professional growth of the teachers and administrators. In this excerpt, I will reflect on my experiences and insights gained from these learning sessions, specifically focusing on the evolution of my understanding of the growth mindset and its impact on my approach to parenting and supporting my child's education.

Before joining the learning journey at Mason Crest with their staff, I had a basic understanding of the growth mindset. However, reading the book and engaging in activities with the Mason Crest staff deepened my comprehension and made my parenting approach more purposeful and consistent. It was an eye-opening experience to realize that much of my instinctive parenting aligns with the principles of a growth mindset. The sessions helped me apply this mindset explicitly to my children's elementary education and further reinforced the importance of embracing mistakes and failures as valuable learning opportunities.

While the learning sessions did not significantly shift my mindset, they reminded me that parenting is an ongoing

---

60. Miracle, Sandra, *Mindset* response, personal communication, July 23, 2023.

learning curve. Embracing mistakes as necessary diagnostic and learning tools allowed me to become a better parent and model the behavior and approach we encouraged our children to embrace. This approach created a team relationship between me and my child, fostering understanding, patience, and empathy. I realized that mistakes and failures are not to be feared but seen as normal parts of the learning process, providing important lessons for both the child and the parent.

Two concepts discussed during the sessions deeply resonated with me as a parent. The first concept is the idea of "You haven't mastered it 'yet.'" This teaches children that not everything comes easily or quickly, instilling persistence and a strong work ethic. It also alleviates their concerns about measuring up to their peers. The second concept is recognizing that mistakes and failures are not inherently bad things. This mindset shift is crucial, allowing for equal learning opportunities from successes and failures. It helps remove the fear of failure and fosters a constructive approach to setbacks.

I envisioned incorporating the principles of a growth mindset into my interactions with my child at home by mirroring the language used by the Mason Crest staff. When the school and parents speak with one voice on issues related to a growth mindset, both parties gain credibility, avoid conflicting messages, and provide consistent lessons about the student's worth, capability, and character. This collaborative approach reinforces the importance of a growth mindset and creates a supportive environment for children to develop and thrive.

The partnership between parents and the Mason Crest staff holds immense potential for further enhancing the implementation of a growth mindset in the school and other schools my children may attend. By teaching parents about growth mindset from the elementary level, the expectation of fostering a growth mindset can continue throughout their K-12 educational journey. Parents can become advocates for growth mindset principles and work collaboratively with teachers and administrators to ensure a consistent and effective approach.

I am VERY frustrated by the lack of coordination with parents throughout the educational system. Schools often communicate primarily with students, leaving parents out of meaningful discussions and decision-making processes. This lack of engagement hinders parents' ability to be actively involved in their children's education. However, the Growth Mindset learning sessions at Mason Crest provided a glimpse into the collaborative educational process that should be more prevalent. It went beyond mindset work, allowing parents to understand teachers' and administrators' challenges and become ambassadors for the school community. Building trust and relationships between parents and educators is essential for effective collaboration and fostering a more comprehensive educational experience.

Participating in the learning sessions with the Mason Crest Elementary School staff was a valuable and transformative experience for me as a parent. It offered a rare opportunity for collaboration and a deeper understanding of the challenges faced by educators. Beyond the growth mindset work, these sessions fostered trust, engagement, and dialogue between parents and the school community. I hope such collaborative efforts become more prevalent across the educational system, promoting a shared vision and a more holistic approach to nurturing our children's academic and personal growth. The importance of parental involvement and effective communication cannot be overstated, and it is essential for schools to actively engage and collaborate with parents to create a thriving educational environment.[61]

---

61. Rockenbach, Richard, *Mindset* response, personal communication, June 23, 2023.

Thought Spark Questions: Growth Mindset and Engaging Parents

How can we address and overcome our own fixed mindset tendencies as educators to effectively teach students about the power of having a growth mindset?

How can we actively involve parents in our approach to learning and foster a shared understanding of the growth mindset philosophy?

What strategies can we implement to invite parents to join us in professional learning sessions and become advocates for the growth mindset philosophy?

How can we cultivate a culture of possibilities, optimism, and belief in our students' unlimited potential by adopting a growth mindset?

How can we create engaging and interactive learning sessions where staff members and parents can share their thoughts, observations, and questions about growth mindset?

How can we collaborate with parents to support each other and help more students succeed?

How can we enhance the implementation of a growth mindset throughout the Pre-K-12 educational journey by involving parents consistently and authentically?

Reflecting on the experiences of Monica Buckhorn, Sandra Miracle, and Richard Rockenbach, how can we create a series of professional learning sessions or workshops based on a growth mindset book or resource? What topics and concepts related to mindset can we explore to deepen our understanding as educators?

Student Goal Setting:
A Powerful Tool to Support a Growth Mindset

Student goal setting is defining and pursuing personal, academic, and career objectives with intention and purpose. It involves identifying aspirations, breaking them into actionable steps, and monitoring progress toward their achievement. As teachers, we can encourage students to set meaningful goals by helping them reflect on their strengths, interests, and areas for growth. By fostering student goal setting, we empower students to take ownership of their learning journey, develop self-motivation, and cultivate a growth mindset.

During our journey at Mason Crest, we explored the concept of growth mindset and discovered valuable strategies to support students in developing their mindset, beliefs, and expectations. One key idea we introduced was the importance of setting goals. However, some staff members initially hesitated, believing that students might be too young for this challenge.

Fortunately, our reading and mathematics coaches—Jacquie Heller, Stacey Duff, Tracey Hulen, and Jenn Deinhart—played a pivotal role in leading our staff through this process. Jacquie explains how our primary grade teachers took the initiative and embraced the goal-setting approach. Their enthusiasm and success in implementing it served as inspiration for the rest of the team.

Jacquie Heller: Goal Setting and Student Goal Cards

We wanted to explore effective ways to provide feedback to students, motivate them, and make them aware of their learning targets. One quote resonated with us. "A student can hit any target as long as they know what it is and it holds still for them," Becky (DuFour) used to say. This led us to consider how we could share these learning targets with students, and we came up with the idea of using goal cards.

We initially implemented this strategy with our kindergarten students, gradually spreading it to first, second, third, fourth, and fifth grades. Each student utilized the goal cards in various content areas. The process involves taking a learning standard, breaking it down into specific learning targets and a learning progression, and then printing it on a piece of card stock, which is then cut up to resemble a bookmark. We also added visuals that were meaningful to the students.

We were particularly focused on nurturing a growth mindset, so we included a creepy brain image that resonated with our first-grade team. They used it to teach students they can grow their brains by engaging in specific actions. Additionally, the flower image aligned with a science unit, conveying that growth occurs over time, just like a seed transforming into a sprout and eventually blooming. The underlying lesson was that where students start doesn't matter; their progress matters. As teachers, our role is to meet them where they are and move them forward.

The versatility of these goal cards is remarkable, as they can be utilized in various environments. In a virtual setting, they can be displayed on the screen to remind students of their targets. They can be used for assessment during conferencing, allowing students to see their progress on the goal cards visually. When used in person, our teachers employed a star-shaped hole punch from a craft store to mark new goals achieved by students. Over time, we made adaptations, such as changing the star symbol to a box for literacy standards that require ongoing practice at more complex text levels. Teachers would mark the box whenever they observed evidence of students employing the targeted strategies.

These goal cards are incredibly flexible and can motivate, engage, assess, and provide feedback. They can also be shared with parents to ensure they understand their child's progress and goals clearly.[62]

Thought Spark Questions: Student Goal Setting and Growth Mindset

1. How can we support students of all grade levels in setting meaningful goals aligned with their personal, academic, and career aspirations?

2. In what ways can we foster a growth mindset among students by emphasizing the importance of effort, strategies, and the learning process in goal pursuit?

3. How can we effectively utilize goal cards or visual tools to make learning targets and progress visible to students? How can these tools be adapted to different grade levels and learning environments?

4. How can we involve parents in understanding and supporting their child's goals through clear and effective communication, such as through the use of goal cards or other means?

---

62. Heller, Jacquie, Question and answer session with Clear Lake School District, March 11, 2021.

5. How can we incorporate knowledge about the brain's potential for growth and learning into our instruction and discussions to enhance students' understanding of goal setting and the development of a growth mindset?

Make It Happen? What Can You Do Today?

- ☐ Present students with information on the brain and its vast potential, including how the brain learns.

- ☐ Praise for strategies, effort, and processes rather than for intelligence or ability.

- ☐ Positive stories provide people with role models of those individuals who have succeeded because of a growth mindset.

- ☐ Writing about your growth mindset experiences to convince others will deepen your growth mindset.

In Chapter 1, we have explored the fascinating world of the brain, movement, relationships, and mindset, uncovering the truth about the unlimited potential within each student. We have delved into the concept of fixed intelligence and challenged its validity, embracing the power of a growth mindset.

However, our journey does not end here. The first step is acquiring knowledge about the fallacy of fixed intelligence and the importance of a growth mindset. We must now confront a significant challenge that lies ahead—the pervasive use of unproductive and marginalizing labels that categorize students.

In Chapter 2, titled **Labels Be Gone**, we will examine these labels' detrimental consequences and their profound impact on our beliefs, expectations, and actions. We will confront the uncomfortable truth that even with the best intentions, well-meaning teachers, administrators, and parents may unknowingly perpetuate these limiting labels.

Chapter 2 is not about dwelling on mistakes or assigning blame. It is about empowering and holding ourselves accountable for creating a better educational environment. We will explore strategies to shed these labels and replace them with a new way of thinking and practicing.

In our understanding, just as sanding and patching walls prepare them for a fresh coat of paint, Chapter 2 acts as the foundation to smooth any rough patches. It will equip us with the tools and insights needed to challenge the prevailing mindset of labeling students and embark on a transformative journey of inclusivity, empowerment, and unlocking the unlimited potential within each student.

So, as we turn the page and embrace Shift #2—"Labels Be Gone"—let us be ready to explore a new way of thinking, a new way of practicing, and a new way of creating an environment where all students can thrive. Together, we can break free from the limitations of labels and pave the way for a brighter future in education.

Possible Answers to Scenarios on Parts of the Brain

Scenario #1

Which two parts of the brain would you be using if you were talking to your friend and riding a skateboard? Can you identify the two areas that could work together?

Possible Answer

Your cerebrum would help you listen and speak while your cerebellum would help you balance.

Scenario #2

Which two parts of the brain would you be using if you were trying to remember something your friend said while you decided whether you wanted a banana or watermelon for a snack?

Possible Answer

Your hippocampus would help you recall the memory, and your pre-frontal cortex would help decide which snack you want.

Scenario #3

Which two parts of the brain would you use if you were looking at your phone and tracking the taxi/rideshare car while feeling stressed that you would be late?

Possible Answer

Your cerebrum would help you look at your phone while your amygdala is activated because of the stress you were feeling (emotions).

CHAPTER 2

L = Labels Be Gone

"The words you speak become the house you live in!"
—Hafiz[63]

He Is a "Problem"

This student resided in the "inner city" within one of the country's most "challenging urban" school systems. During eighth grade, he consistently skipped school, causing his "single mother" to feel helpless. Consequently, she sent him to live with his aunt in a different part of the country. His new destination was an "affluent high school within one of the nation's top school districts." To support students who had not succeeded in eighth grade, the school had implemented a program that allowed them to retake the eighth-grade requirements they had "failed" while concurrently enrolling in some ninth-grade classes. Upon reviewing the student's transcript and learning about his previous city and school system, one educator in the room impulsively exclaimed to her colleagues, "He is a problem."

Please reflect on the passage above and consider the words or phrases in parentheses. Do these words or phrases evoke a negative or positive perception or portray the student in a problematic light? Has the student

63. "The Words You Speak Become the House You Live In," Spiralup, https://spiralup.com/words-speak-become-house-live/#:~:text=%E2%80%9CThe%20words%20you%20speak%20become,in.%E2%80%9D%20%E2%80%93Attributed%20to%20Hafiz&text=Words%20are%20the%20building%20blocks,his%20research%20in%20cell%20physiology.

already been labeled? What about the phrase "affluent high school situated within one of the nation's top school districts?" What picture instantly comes to mind?

What conscious and unconscious beliefs and expectations might arise regarding this student? Have assumptions about the student already transformed into expectations?

Fortunately, those in the room rebelled against such labeling and began considering the possibilities. Rather than judging the student based on his transcript and assuming he would be troublesome, many in the room believed he deserved a fresh start. When the student finally arrived, he was nothing like the image painted by his transcript. His genuine personality shone through—friendly, outgoing, courteous, and respectful.

The rest is history. This student excelled in sports at his new school. The people around him genuinely wanted to support him, and even if he had displayed less agreeable qualities, the individuals in the room were ready to assist him. However, the student did not match the person described on paper.

We must exercise caution when judging students based on their "reputation" or transcripts. They are not defined solely by external factors. If we embrace a growth mindset and believe in people's capacity to change and improve, our efforts should focus on helping them do just that. In this case, the student secured a full sports scholarship, graduated from college, and now owns a successful company operating in the United States and other countries. Consider this momentarily: If the people in the room had remained silent or inactive when the educator labeled him a "problem," the young man's future would have been drastically different. Educators must perceive students as individuals with limitless potential, especially during their school years when their brains are still developing, and their decision-making may not always be rational. We must support and guide them. The label "He is a problem" was the actual problem.

Over the years, I have heard fellow educators express that we are not just making a difference in students' lives—many times, we *are* the difference!

In their book *Removing Labels*, Smith, Fisher, and Frey wrote:

> We telegraph our expectations of students in a myriad of ways. Our interactions with students and our willingness to demand more or less of them come through verbally and non-verbally. Another seminal study in education demonstrated how teacher interactions telegraphed these expectations to students. Good (1987) chronicled how teacher expectations translated into observable differential interactions depending on whether the teacher perceived students as high- or low-achieving. In particular, students perceived as low achieving:
>
> - are criticized more often for failure,
> - are praised less frequently,
> - receive less feedback,
> - are called on less often,
> - are seated farther away from the teacher,
> - have less eye contact from the teacher,
> - have fewer friendly interactions with the teacher, and
> - experience acceptance of their ideas less often.[64]

In essence, that one educator's statement about the student she called "a problem" could have set him up for failure and a genuinely negative experience in that school if the rest of the people around her agreed. This student's future, as education author Mike Mattos states,

---

64. Smith, Dominique, Fisher, Douglas, and Frey, Nancy, *Removing Labels*, Corwin, 2001, pp. 5-6.

whose life was "filled with endless opportunities and possibilities,"[65] could have ended right there, at the moment that educator made the negative and biased statement, if the other people in that room had agreed.

I found a quote I often use that gives people the courage to speak up when a colleague or colleagues begin to speak negatively about a student.

"When the stories about a student are saturated with negativity, have the courage to not join in. Tell a new story of their unique abilities and moments of kindness. Tell a story of hope."[66]

The labeling of students is so pernicious in our schools that we do not even think about it and its adverse effects very much. It is a habit ingrained in our culture, the way we do business. The idea of labeling students with these negative labels must go. Words do matter! In their book *Starting a Movement*, Ken Williams and Tom Hierck write, *"Labels often begin as identifiers of how people are incidentally different, but over time these labels begin to represent something more than identification and support labels begin to damage those they identify, and we lower expectations."*[67]

Ken Williams has a YouTube video entitled "Are You Teaching Students or Labels?" In the video, Ken says:

A step toward equity is we got to stop teaching labels and start teaching students. Why would we expect the best from our students, the best version of themselves, when we have tattooed them with these marginalizing labels? Why would we expect their best? I would not get your best [educators] if I started [by saying] I need you to rearrange yourselves… [in] high, medium,

65. Mattos, Mike, "When All Means All," Keynote PLC at Work Institute, San Antonio, TX, July 2016.

66. Author unknown.

67. Williams, Ken and Hierck, Tom, *Starting a Movement: Building Culture from the Inside Out in Professional Learning Communities*, Solution Tree Press, 2015, pp. 10-11.

and low ability [teacher] groups. I would not get the best version of you today so why should we expect it from kids?

It's one thing to meet them where they are and take them where they need to go; it's another thing to meet them where you have put them. When I went to school the kids who were considered low were low all the way through, the kids who were considered average were average all the way through, and the kids educators considered smart were smart all the way through. Opportunities and access were all impacted by these decisions.

We have got to do better because where they go is based on you [educators]. That's why I'm done talking about demographics and population as a reason why students aren't learning. I just work with the adults and typically after a couple of hours, I have a pretty good idea whether the expertise and talent are assembled in the room. That's what it comes down to! That is what it comes down to.[68]

In my conversation with assessment and grading expert Tom Schimmer on his podcast, Tom said this about labeling students:

I think sometimes we get locked into those labels. I saw that in my jurisdiction as well where especially with behavioral designations and identifiers where they're supposed to be temporary, they're supposed to work to help the student learn the social skills and yet they become a life sentence. Then they become sort of this category of students that everybody becomes cautious about. We start to have different inferences and different nonverbal reactions and all sorts of things surrounding those labels. They tend to be triggers for people and it's unfortunate because it spirals out of control and next thing you know we've got someone labeled and locked in a

68. Unfold The Soul, "Are You Teaching Students Or Labels," YouTube, https://www. youtube.com/watch?v=1Gyr-490BX8.

box. We don't necessarily even attempt to help transition them to learn the social skills or learn the academic skills that would take them out of that label.[69]

Throughout my career as an educator, I have seen many people label students using different terms, and I do not think they necessarily mean to do the student harm. However, they do not realize that the more they use these labels, the more they adhere to this self-fulfilling prophecy and teach to that label. I have used labels during my career as well. I am not going to sit here and say I am perfect, but I started to realize that the more I used those labels, those words, these marginalizing terms, the more I started to believe that the label was the student. Jeanne Spiller and I wrote an article blog on this subject in January 2020 entitled "Labels Be Gone." The adapted article below shares our mindshift and practice change around labeling students.

Does All Mean All?

LABELS BE GONE
By Jeanne Spiller and Brian Butler

Courtesy of Kenneth Williams Defenders and Disruptors of the Status Quo - Who Will Educators Choose To Be... 2017

---

69. Tom Schimmer Podcast, "Brian Butler (Ep. 51 - Tom Schimmer Podcast)," YouTube, 2021, https://www.youtube.com/watch?v=M4_rDTpvHK8.

Great teachers who truly want what is best for their students sometimes engage in this behavior. Principals and parents who care deeply about what is best for students also engage in this behavior. We have too and meant no harm. It happens and we all need to be more cognizant of the implications. So, what is this behavior? This behavior is summing up or labeling students in one word or with phrases like the ones in the visual above.

Our assumptions drive our actions. What if we as a profession heeded the research from Wendy Berliner, who said, "The latest neuroscience and psychological research suggest most people unless they are cognitively impaired, can reach standards of performance associated with gifted and talented" students.[70] What if we truly embrace, advocate for, and protect the following mindsets?

1) **We assume that All students CAN learn at high levels.**

2) **We accept responsibility to ENSURE that all students learn at high levels—Grade level or better.**

These are often the mindsets that frame many of our district or school mission statements. How can we fully embrace these mindsets when we use terms like the ones shared above, or we say things like "he is one of my high kids," "I have a really low class this year," or "she is one of my sweet and lows."

A Few Reasons Why We May Engage in Labeling Students

1. We believe the label will help the student get what he/she needs. Specialized support may be provided because of the label.

---

70. "Why there's no such thing as a gifted child," *The Guardian*, https://www.theguardian.com/education/2017/jul/25/no-such-thing-as-a-gifted-child-einstein-iq.

2. A documented diagnosis and label are often what trigger funding.

3. The label helps explain low performance. It is not us, it is the student, they are not performing because they have special needs, because they are "low," because they have a complicated home life, etc.

4. We truly want what we think is best for the student. We want to help them.

While some of the reasons are valid, and may help provide services the student needs, we often find that the labels provide a convenient excuse for low expectations and performance. Instead of making excuses, we should ask ourselves how we can contribute to ensuring that each student learns essential grade-level concepts and partner with specialized service providers to ensure student success.

Why Labeling Can Be Harmful

The qualifier or label is not who the student is, it merely indicates something the student may need or identifies circumstances the student may be currently experiencing. If we are not careful, we can subconsciously attribute a set of expectations to the label. "Oh, he is a special education student, there is no way he can master that standard, we should give him something easier that he can handle," or "she's a really low reader, she can't read grade-level text, let's find text she can read instead." What if we provided strategies and scaffolds for students to access grade-level material instead? These scenarios play out in schools every day, and we believe contribute to the achievement gaps that exist in most schools.

Many years ago, when we began our professional careers as educators, we both engaged in labeling students and recall that we indeed had higher expectations for those we labeled as high achievers and lower expectations for those we labeled as low achievers. We had confidence in the high achievers and challenged them often. We had less confidence in those we labeled as low (many times unconsciously) and didn't push them or challenge them as much. We understand now that we were also sending an unintended message to students that we believed in them, or we didn't, and that realization was very difficult for both of us. We had good intentions. We did this because we truly cared about our students and did not want some students to unnecessarily struggle. We didn't allow for challenge or productive struggle, in fact, we shielded them from it. We understand now that all students benefit from challenge, high expectations and productive struggle, and we do better now, but we often wish we could go back and do it all over again with high expectations for all no matter what!

Our profession can be very difficult. We have a wide range of students with differing learning needs, and it is our job to ensure that they are all as successful as possible. As we navigate the challenge of meeting the needs of a diverse student body, we must be aware of our unconscious bias and stop looking out the window for the reasons or excuses to explain away why students may not be reaching high levels of learning and instead start looking in the mirror to determine how we can empower students to overcome obstacles and succeed despite any circumstance they face. We don't have to figure this out alone. It's easy to get frustrated and fall into the habit of labeling students when we work in isolation and cannot tap into our colleagues' collective knowledge and talents if we don't work in a collaborative culture to help elevate our practice and stimulate new thinking and instructional strategies.

How Collaborative Teams Can Help Us

When teachers work together on collaborative teams focused on high levels of learning for all students, we promote feelings of collective efficacy. In other words, our actions can make a difference for our students, and with our guidance and support, all our students will learn grade-level expectations. As members of collaborative teams, we can remind each other that learning is our fundamental purpose. We can use evidence of learning to celebrate growth and to determine appropriate instruction and intervention for students who need support. Together, we can determine the best ways to overcome the barriers to learning, find student strengths and capitalize on them, and work to ensure that students are confident learners who believe they are capable.

In John Hattie's exhaustive meta-analysis in which he ranked factors that affect student achievement, teacher Collective Efficacy had the highest effect size of 1.57. The average effect size is .40. This amounts to multiple years of growth within a single year for students. In the article "The Power of Collective Efficacy," Hattie et al write, "Success lies in the critical nature of collaboration and the strength of believing that together, administrators, faculty, and students can accomplish great things." This is the power of collective efficacy. "When efficacy is present in a school culture, educators' efforts are enhanced—especially when they are faced with difficult challenges. Since expectations for success are high, teachers and leaders approach their work with an intensified persistence and strong resolve....collective efficacy influences student achievement indirectly through productive patterns of teaching behavior."[71]

---

71. Donohoo, Jenni, Hattie, John, and Eells, Rachel, "The Power of Collective Efficacy," *Educational Leadership*, March 2018.

We have both been a part of model PLC at Work Schools and Districts and have witnessed the power of collective efficacy and how teachers benefit from being a part of a true collaborative team. Being a member of a collaborative team within a PLC at Work School will give teachers access to more tools. Being a part of an effective team will make teachers mutually accountable to each other and compel educators to look in the mirror at the most important factor for that student to ensure that they focus on achieving the goal of learning for all.[72]

In the book *Removing the Mask: Giftedness in Poverty*, Slocumb and Payne write:

The sources of inequity for students from poverty are rooted in the home and the resources available to the student. Access to these resources increases the probability that young children will perform better in school. These resources within the home are vital to the student's skills, attitudes, and motivation.... These resources, or lack thereof, contribute significantly to the opportunities that students do or do not have in their formative years. Impoverished backgrounds contribute to lesser skill and lower production levels. This "lack of" is clearly and most definitely judged in school settings.[73]

72. Spiller, Jeanne and Butler, Brian, "Does All Mean All? Labels Be Gone!" https://www.allthingsplc.info/blog/view/409/does-all-mean-all-labels-be-gone.

73. Slocumb, Paul D. and Payne, Ruby, *Removing the Mask: Giftedness in Poverty*, Aha Process, 2000, pp. 9-10.

Two Children Born on the Same Day in the Same Hospital

TWO DIFFERENT LABELS—TWO DIFFERENT FUTURES?

"Strengths (or talents) are an outgrowth of interest activated by exposure and practice. Identifying and activating student strengths encourages students' belief in their potential."

—Yvette Jackson[74]

Let's look at it differently with two students born on the same day and in the same hospital. We will call them Child A and Child B. Consider this scenario. Child A and Child B were born on the same day in the same hospital, setting the stage for an intriguing comparison. Their early childhood experiences diverged significantly, shaping their journeys into kindergarten.

Child A was fortunate enough to attend a high-quality play-based preschool, surrounded by engaging activities that fostered their development. Child A's parents had flexible work schedules and devoted time to reading to Child A every night. The child's life was filled with opportunities for growth, including participation in various extracurricular activities such as dance classes, soccer, basketball, and swim lessons. Child A's parents took them on numerous adventures, both near and far, exposing them to diverse experiences and opening their horizons. By the time Child A entered kindergarten, they had been exposed to many enriching experiences, sparking their curiosity and allowing them to explore their interests. The child's parents, both college graduates and financially secure, nurtured Child A's talents and strengths that had emerged from this supportive environment.

In contrast, Child B faced different circumstances. Their parents worked tirelessly, juggling multiple jobs to make ends meet, resulting in a combined income of less than $65,000 per year for a family of five. Preschool was not an option for Child B, and when the child fell ill,

---

74. Jackson, Yvette. *The Pedagogy of Confidence.* Teachers College Press, 2011, p. 91.

their parents could not take time off work, leaving their older siblings to miss school and care for Child B. Opportunities for extracurricular activities were scarce, and the family could not embark on adventures or travel extensively. Child B's exposure to enriching experiences was limited, hindering their ability to discover their interests and strengths. As they entered kindergarten, Child B lagged behind their peers. The teacher noted their struggle to follow class rules, lack of familiarity with letters and numbers, and difficulties with basic motor skills like correctly holding a pencil or crayon.

The teacher's initial observations painted a stark contrast between Child A and Child B. Child A seemed advanced, having excelled in various areas, while Child B appeared to be falling behind. However, the situation was more complex than it seemed.

Both Child A and Child B had unique gifts and unlimited potential. Child A's achievements were a result of the supportive environment and opportunities provided by their parents, while Child B's lack of exposure hindered their progress. It was essential to recognize that Child B was not a slow learner but simply had not yet had the chance to explore and discover their strengths.

Rather than labeling one child as gifted and the other as lacking, it was crucial to maintain high expectations for both students, independent of their family backgrounds. Child A's advanced abilities should be acknowledged and challenged further, while Child B needs additional support to bridge the gaps caused by their limited experiences. With time and appropriate assistance, Child B would catch up, as their talents and interests were waiting to be activated.

The teacher and the educational system needed to recognize that every child has unlimited potential and should be given opportunities to flourish, regardless of their circumstances. Child B might not be "there yet," but with patience, support, and equal expectations, they would uncover their unique gifts and talents. It was a matter of providing the necessary time and resources for Child B to develop and grow, just as Child A had been given from the beginning.

In the end, the story of Child A and Child B highlighted the importance of nurturing every child's unlimited potential, irrespective of their background, and ensuring that a wide range of opportunities were accessible to all.

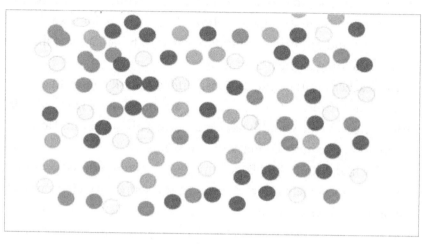

Dots denote enriching opportunities Child A is afforded each year until entering kindergarten.

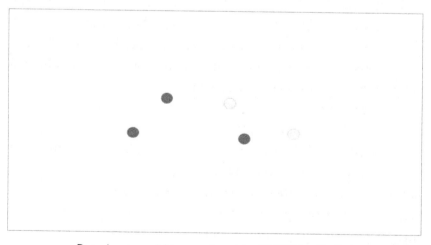

Dots denote enriching opportunities Child B is afforded each year until entering kindergarten

If you were advising the teacher, what would you share about Child A and Child B and how to move forward? Remember the quote from Yvette Jackson that started this section: *"Strengths (or talents) are an outgrowth of interest activated by exposure and practice. Identifying and activating student strengths encourages students' belief in their potential."*

I was born into a middle-class home with ample opportunities and college-educated parents, granting me an advantage. Despite this, I faced challenges in developing fluent reading skills and lacked confidence as a learner. However, I was fortunate to have supportive parents who helped me, with my dad occasionally assisting me with my homework assignments. I did not experience a "lack of" resources; my privileged upbringing sometimes concealed the extent of my struggles in school. This realization often leads me to wonder where I would be today if I had been born into a different home with fewer opportunities.

"Stella, you are so talented. I know you will always do well!"

"So telling children they're smart, in the end, made them feel dumber, but claim they were smarter. I don't think this is what we're aiming for when we put positive labels—'gifted,' 'talented,' and 'brilliant'—on people. We don't mean to rob them of their zest for challenge and their recipes for Success...This is the danger of positive labels."
—CAROL DWECK[75]

75. Dweck, Carol, *Mindset the New Psychology of Success*, Ballantine, 2006, p. 74.

Stella's parents had a laid-back approach, aiming to give her every opportunity they could afford. At nine, Stella displayed exceptional golf skills, not because she was inherently more gifted than other children who had never played, but due to her opportunities and extensive practice with the feedback she had received. Stella's golf journey began when her father placed a putter in her hands at two years of age. Subsequently, she started accompanying her father and older brother to the golf range.

Stella found joy in hitting golf balls, and being around her family made it even more special. By the time she reached six or seven years old, it was estimated that Stella had hit over ten thousand golf balls on the range and practiced putting a golf ball thousands of times. Eventually, her parents arranged for Stella to have a coach. Stella, who had perfectionistic tendencies, who disliked making mistakes or losing, might have developed this mindset from wanting to match the skill level of her brother who was four years older.

Around the same time, when Stella was six or seven, her parents enrolled her in golf tournaments. Before her first tournament, Stella felt highly anxious, and, unfortunately, she came in last place. This outcome devastated her as she believed she did not live up to the positive label of being "so talented" that everyone had given her since she started playing golf. Stella considered quitting the sport.

Considering what you know now about labels, the brain, and mindset from Chapters 1 and 2, reflect on and answer the following questions about Stella:

- What are some reasons (without placing blame) for Stella's meltdown?

- What could have been done to support Stella's perfectionistic tendencies?

- What can be done now to support Stella?

- Why can positive labels about talent (such as constantly telling Stella she was "so talented" at golf) be just as detrimental as negative labels, like considering oneself a terrible golfer?

The Rest of the Story

Stella's parents recognized the need to act. They did not want her to quit golf, but they didn't want to force her to play either. They understood her love for the sport and wanted to equip her with the necessary tools to persevere. They introduced her to the concept of a growth mindset, aiming to help her embrace challenges and view them as opportunities for improvement. Stella's parents believed that persisting was a skill applicable to golf and a valuable life skill. They wanted her to understand that effort would lead to improvement. Learning from feedback provided by her coach, parents, peers, and herself would help her progress. Moreover, observing successful golfers, including her brother and father, would be positive models for her golfing journey. They shared videos with Stella, helping her comprehend the game of golf and learn from the perseverance and practice exhibited by other accomplished golfers in tournaments.

Stella's parents clarified that their only desire was for her to find happiness and enjoyment in the game. They emphasized that focused and enjoyable practice would lead to more enjoyment as she improved. As mentioned in the previous chapter, neurotransmitters in the brain affect our emotions. When Stella wanted to quit, cortisol, the stress hormone, was activated, likely putting her in flight mode. The objective was to activate her prefrontal cortex, the part of the brain responsible for critical thinking and decision-making, to trigger the release of "happy chemicals." By persisting and practicing, Stella would experience the positive feelings associated with dopamine and other "happy chemicals."

Stella's parents continued to guide her, assuring her that it was acceptable not to succeed every time. They taught her about the brain and introduced breathing exercises to help her calm her mind. Her coach taught her visualization techniques and mental rehearsal of golf shots, encouraging positive thinking about the outcomes. They helped her understand the challenges that amateur and professional golfers face. Stella's parents and coach showed her videos of professional golfers making mistakes and how they responded. They also took her to a professional women's golf tournament. They worked with her on a process of reflection, a quick analysis of mistakes, correcting them, and moving on to the next shot.

Due to the observation of Stella's perfectionistic tendencies in other areas, her parents sought assistance from the school. Fortunately, the school had recently adopted a growth mindset philosophy and had begun teaching it to all students. Stella's parents inquired if any techniques used in school could support Stella in golf and at home. The school provided them with talking points and mindset sentence frames to assist her when she felt anxious or believed she could not overcome challenges because they seemed too difficult.

Growth Mindset Sentence Frames for Stella

- I like that you took on that challenging golf hole, Stella.
- I am excited to see you stretching yourself and working to improve your putting.
- I admire the way you concentrated after that unfortunate shot.
- You put so much thought into this.
- The passion and effort you put into practicing and improving bring me joy. How do you feel about it?
- Whoops, practicing putting from this short distance was too easy. I apologize for wasting your time. Let's increase the distance so you can truly master putts from four to six feet.
- I can see how hard you are working. You must feel proud of yourself.
- Your dedication to practicing with the 3-wood and driver is commendable.
- I appreciate your effort, but let's continue working together to make your short irons more consistent.

- It may take more time to become comfortable hitting a fairway wood, but you'll get there with persistence.

- Every athlete has a unique approach to the game of golf. Let's keep trying to find the approach that works best for you.

- I'm proud of your commitment to improvement.

- It upsets me when you don't finish what you started. Nobody hits a great shot every time or wins all matches, but finishing is important.

- We can tackle challenging tasks.

This dedicated effort in teaching Stella about her brain and the growth mindset began to yield positive results. Stella developed a much more positive outlook on golf and started enjoying the hard work that came with it. She embraced playing and improving in tournaments, focusing less on her score and less on winning. Something unique started to happen: Stella became a role model for her peers on the course, gently helping them with their mindsets using the Growth Mindset Sentence Statements the adults had used with her. As a result, Stella began winning a few tournaments and even received an invitation to a major junior tournament because of her positive attitude and solid play.

To conclude Stella's story, let us reference another quote from Carol Dweck: *"I think educators commonly hold two beliefs that do just that. Many believe that (1) praising students' intelligence builds their confidence and motivation to learn, and (2) students' inherent intelligence is the major cause of their achievement in school. Our research has shown that the first belief is false and that the second can be harmful—even for the most competent students."*[76]

---

76. Dweck, Carol, "The Perils and Promise of Praise," ASCD, October 1, 2007, https://www.ascd.org/el/articles/the-perils-and-promises-of-praise.

Label the Skill, Not the Person

Label the skill, not the student or person! When Stella was given the label of *highly talented or so good*, she felt an immense amount of pressure to live up to that label. How do we eliminate some negative or positive labels that can be harmful? Well, start here. Try one week as a label-free zone. In the one-week challenge, write it down and put it in a jar every time you use one of the marginalizing terms below or any of the terms you've seen or used before.

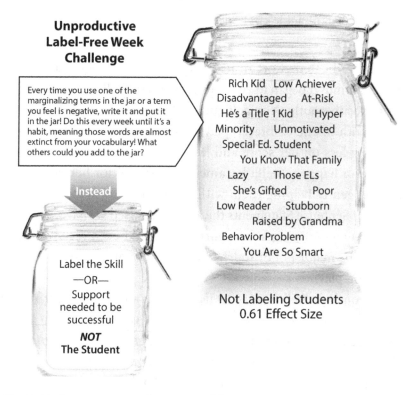

Unproductive Label-Free Week Challenge

Every time you use one of the marginalizing terms in the jar or a term you feel is negative, write it and put it in the jar! Do this every week until it's a habit, meaning those words are almost extinct from your vocabulary! What others could you add to the jar?

Instead

Rich Kid   Low Achiever
Disadvantaged   At-Risk
He's a Title 1 Kid   Hyper
Minority   Unmotivated
Special Ed. Student
      You Know That Family
Lazy   Those ELs
      She's Gifted   Poor
Low Reader   Stubborn
      Raised by Grandma
Behavior Problem
      You Are So Smart

Label the Skill
—OR—
Support needed to be successful
NOT
The Student

Not Labeling Students
0.61 Effect Size

Yvette Jackson suggests that we could use more appropriate positive terms instead of a negative or marginalizing label. For example, instead of using **minority**, use **students of color or no classification**. Instead of **using low achievers**, use **underachievers**. Instead of **disadvantaged**, use **school dependent**.[77]

77. Jackson, Yvette and Feuerstein, Reuven, *The Pedagogy of Confidence Inspiring High Intellectual Performance in Urban Schools*, Teachers College Press, 2011, pp. 20-21.

As author Lee Ann Jung has posted on social media, *"Students who have IEPs are not 'special education students.' They are just students. They belong to every teacher they have. Receiving a service does not change a student's identity..."*[78] Instead of **special education students**, use **general education students receiving special education services**.

Remember, we are not labeling the student; we are labeling the skill or the service. Not labeling students has a positive .61 effect size on student achievement.[79] One year's growth is a .40 with the average teacher.

My Name Is My Most Important and Positive Label

WHEN WE HAVE DIFFICULTY PRONOUNCING A STUDENT'S NAME, GIVING THEM A NICKNAME IS AN UNINTENTIONAL LABEL!

What does this have to do with labels? It has everything to do with labels, although it may be unintentional. When I started my career, I sometimes heard an audible groan when teachers got their student roster. A few would look at the students' names and say, "I do not know how to say that. I am going to shorten that name, or I am going to change that name. I'm going to give them a nickname." Think about that! Learning a student's name is the foundation of relationship building. Addressing a student by their name, by their correct name, is a sign of respect! It's saying you know who they are! A person's name is central to their identity, so we must take the time to learn a student's name correctly.

When a student comes in in Pre-K and kindergarten and first grade all the way through, if we change their name or shorten their name or give them a nickname, we are telling that student that their being is unimportant. We're treating them as others, as different than those in their classroom. This is central to what we do when we first learn about or meet a student. Learning a student's name promotes trustworthiness and the element of

---

78. Jung, Lee Ann, @leeannjung, "Students who have IEPs are not special education students," Twitter, November 20, 2022.

79. Hattie, John, "Global research database," Visible Learning MetaX, https://www.visiblelearningmetax.com/influences.

teacher credibility. Teacher credibility is a student's perception of whether they can learn from you. This is a whopping 1.09 effect size.[80]

When students come into our schools, are we taking time to make sure that we are saying their names correctly? If you do not know how to say their name, ask them. There are several name games that we can play, and there are several resources, tools, and strategies that we can use to learn a student's name, but this is critical.

Over the years as an educator, I would have so many students come up to me and ask, "Mr. Butler, do you know my name?" There were times when I would forget, but I would try to ask them and to ask them to tell me about their name. Knowing somebody's name is central to who they are.

People have asked me if it is okay once you have established a trusting relationship to give a student a nickname. My general response is that I am okay with that, but the first thing we do is we want to make sure that we know and learn their name correctly, and we can say it because that gives you credibility. When you build that relationship, and you're comfortable, and they are comfortable, and if the student says it is okay, yeah, that is fine, but their name is the name they were given at birth. That should be the name that we learned first.

> "Pronouncing students' names correctly is crucial to making them feel included. Our name is our identity; it is tied to our culture and our family history. If we have trouble pronouncing the names correctly, we will need to practice with the student one-on-one. The entire class must be exposed to diverse names and their correct pronunciation."[81]
>
> —MONIQUE ROSKE

80. Hattie, John, "Global research database," Visible Learning MetaX, https://www.visiblelearningmetax.com/influences.

81. Roske, Monique, presentation to Chincoteague Elementary School, personal communication, November 13, 2018.

Make Them Say Your Name

Akbar Gbaja-Biamila is a former National Football League (NFL) player. He is a commentator and co-host on the *American Ninja Warrior* television series and is currently one of the co-hosts of *The Talk* on CBS. On Facebook, he recounted his childhood in LA, where he endured frequent ridicule due to his Nigerian last name. He felt ashamed and yearned for a more conventional name. One day, after being upset by schoolyard taunts, his father told him sternly to make his teachers pronounce his name. Initially intimidated by his father's stern words, a pivotal shift occurred in Akbar's mindset. He resolved to assertively make others pronounce his name, even when teachers attempted to evade it. He transformed the situation from embarrassment to empowerment, determined to no longer be the subject of mockery. This newfound attitude cultivated a sense of pride and ownership in his identity. Inspired by his father's guidance, Akbar harnessed this self-assuredness to excel academically and athletically, and this all happened because his dad told him to make the teachers say his name.

In the article "Why Pronouncing Student Names Correctly Matters, and How to Get Them Right," Lydia McFarlane discusses the "My Name, My Identity" initiative in Santa Clara County, California.[82] Launched in 2016, the initiative is a collaboration between the Santa Clara County Office of Education and the National Association of Bilingual Education. It aims to foster respect for students' names and identities, encompassing over sixty languages spoken by thousands of students in the county.

Through signing the pledge, participants commit to:

1. Properly pronouncing students' names.
2. Serving as role models for others in respecting names and identities.

82. McFarlane, Lydia, "Why Pronouncing Student Names Correctly Matters, and How to Get Them Right," *EdWeek*, July 17, 2023, https://www.edweek.org/leadership/why-pronouncing-student-names-correctly-matters-and-how-to-get-them-right/2023/07.

3. Spreading awareness about the significance of correct name pronunciation.

4. Encouraging the sharing of name stories on social media.

5. Promoting a sense of pride in one's identity.

In Chapter 4, we will explore a powerful teacher strategy aimed at helping all students confront challenges and engage with traditional gifted curriculum. This strategy fosters connections and links learning to empower students through relationships and relevance. Notably, a key element of this strategy involves knowing and correctly pronouncing a student's name, as this simple act enhances a teacher's credibility and enables the effective use of this approach.

Unproductive Practices that Label Students

WHAT CAN WE STOP DOING TODAY?

Before delving into this topic, I asked friends on social media in order to gather insights on Unproductive Practices that Label Students. I asked them to share any practices (anonymously) they have observed or participated in. Their responses shed light on the pervasive nature of labeling in our school culture. While we may not always explicitly use word labels, our actions often indicate that we are unintentionally categorizing and labeling students.

- Always seating the same students with paraeducators/instructional assistants at the back of the room unintentionally stigmatizes and excludes them.

- Exclusively assigning the special education teacher to work only with students with Individual Education Plans (IEPs) creates a perception that these students are separate from the rest of the class.

- Restricting the general education teacher to work solely with students who do not receive special education services implies that other students are exclusively the special education teacher's responsibility.

- Consistently selecting high-scoring students to answer questions or present in front of the class unintentionally reinforces a hierarchical divide among students.

- Using public displays of achievement, such as posting test scores or grades, that label students as "high achievers" or "low achievers" promotes unnecessary comparisons.

- Categorizing students based solely on academic performance or perceived abilities limits their growth potential, and fosters fixed mindset beliefs.

- Overreliance on standardized tests as the primary measure of student ability narrows the perspective on intelligence and disregards other valuable skills.

- Utilizing biased language or stereotypes in feedback or comments about students inadvertently reinforces limiting beliefs and expectations.

- Neglecting to recognize and embrace the diversity of students' backgrounds, experiences, and cultural identities leads to feelings of exclusion and perpetuates stereotypes.

- Placing excessive emphasis on grades and performance outcomes without valuing effort, progress, and personal growth conveys that only academic results matter.

- Failing to provide individualized support and accommodations for students with diverse learning needs hinders their educational progress.

- Overlooking students' strengths and interests outside traditional academic subjects disregards their talents and passions.

- Applying fixed labels or categories to describe students, such as "gifted," "average," or "struggling," can impact self-perception.
- Neglecting opportunities for students to reflect on their learning journey, set goals, and develop a growth mindset hinders their ability to embrace challenges and persevere.

By eliminating these practices, we can create a more inclusive and supportive learning environment that values the unlimited potential and growth of all students, regardless of labels or perceived abilities.

Please continue to add to the list by sharing examples of practices that inadvertently label students.

Who Is The Gifted Label For? And the Children Will Lead

WHY LABELING STUDENTS AS "GIFTED" ISN'T WORKING

In a thought-provoking TED-Ed talk, Ava Echard (2019) shared her journey of being labeled "gifted" at a young age. She raised critical questions about the effectiveness of such categorization.

Ava recalled her experience as a five-year-old, solving puzzles in a small room, unaware of this assessment's long-term impact on her life. Though her parents and the administrator assured her it was all in good fun, they secretly hoped she would excel, recognizing the potential advantages of the "gifted" label.

As she advanced through school, Ava became part of a select group known as the "gifted and talented," where students who performed well on tests were considered above their age level. However, she began to question the true significance of this classification and the meaning of being "gifted."

As Ava and her peers discussed their experiences within the gifted program, they discovered the drawbacks of such labeling. They were placed in a smart kid group, were observed closely for mistakes, and felt compelled to live up to the gifted label. The weight of high expectations led to anxiety and perfectionism, making every failure feel amplified because they were expected to be innately special and always succeed.

Ava then delved into the broader impact of this system on society. She highlighted the racial and socioeconomic disparities in access to gifted education. Students from low-income households, particularly African American and Hispanic students, are less likely to be identified and given the same opportunities.

She questioned whether innate ability determining one's future is valid or whether external factors like race, income, and upbringing influence it. Ava proposed that the circumstances of a child's life play a significant role in their abilities and unlimited potential.

Moreover, she challenged the notion of fixed intelligence, arguing that it expands and contracts based on the challenges individuals seek for themselves. Intelligence should not be confined to academic performance but should encompass curiosity, creativity, and perseverance.

Ava advocated for a change in the education system. She urged educators to trust students with individual large-scale projects based on their interests and not just focus on an advanced curriculum. She suggested eliminating early labeling and offering after-school programs that explore real-world applications and advanced topics.

Ava emphasized creating inclusive learning environments that celebrate diverse interests and foster curiosity, empathy, and creativity in all students. By doing so, she argued that we can break free from the limitations of a narrow definition of intelligence and allow every child to shape their own future.[83]

83. TED-Ed Student Talks, "Why labeling students as 'gifted' isn't working." YouTube, August 2019, https://www.youtube.com/watch?v=Z0LhdQIhmzk.

What We Can Do Moving Forward

What if we walked the talk of our mission statements daily in every school for every student? We must be willing to examine our espoused beliefs and practices to determine if they match. If we say we believe *all* means *all*, then every action we take and every word we utter must be in alignment with that belief. We must have the integrity to protect what we believe is important. As author Brené Brown writes in her book *Rising Strong*, "*Integrity is choosing courage over comfort; choosing what is right over what is fun, fast or easy; and choosing to practice values rather than simply professing them.*"[84]

In a blog post on the site Philippine Basic Education, Angel de Dios wrote:

> Much of what we teachers currently do inside our classroom does not often match how we see ourselves. I do not think we label teachers as "dumb" or "gifted." I do not think teachers think of themselves as individuals having a fixed amount of intelligence. Teachers talk with each other and learn from each other. Teachers practice discipline in their work. Lastly, teachers, I hope, prefer practices or strategies that work. Yet, in most classrooms teachers often do the opposite of these things.
>
> We label kids. We think intelligence is something we cannot nurture. We isolate ourselves. We forget the necessary amount of discipline we knew is crucial for learning. We forget the joy of being curious. We have failed to open our minds to see new strategies that are much more effective. We have failed to embrace the very important principle that education is for all and that all means all. [85]

---

84. Brown, Brené, *Rising Strong: How the Ability to Reset Transforms the Way We Live, Love, Parent, and Lead*, Random House, 2017.

85. de Dios, Angel, "The Way We Teach Should Be the Way We See Ourselves," Philippine Basic Education, November 9, 2021, https://www.philippinesbasiceducation. us/2021/11/the-way-we-teach-should-be-way-we-see.html.

I have consistently asked and will continue to ask: How would we want a teacher to discuss our child? Language can shape our actions, and if we are open to altering our words, thoughts, and methods, we can impact lives. In what way will you fiercely support, champion, and safeguard students with the powerful statement: **LABELS BE GONE!?**

Having addressed the negative impact of marginalizing labels and provided strategies to mitigate their effects in Chapter 2, we now transition to Chapter 3, titled "O = Obligation of Teams." In this chapter, the focus shifts to the power of collective teacher efficacy and collective responsibility, emphasizing the importance of educators embracing vulnerability and sharing our unique strengths, passions, and talents for the good of the student.

Chapter 3 can be likened to the process of priming the walls before painting. Just as priming prepares the walls to absorb better and showcase the paint, this chapter sets the stage for educators to collaborate and leverage their collective expertise, ultimately enhancing the educational experience for all students.

O = Obligation of Teams

*"Value the contributions of all, blending the skills of individual
staff members in unsurpassed collaboration."*
—Mayo Clinic Mission and Values Statement on Teamwork[86]

The Most Significant Challenge

The shift we discuss in this chapter presents the most significant challenge among the five shifts. Why? Because it requires us to transform the culture ingrained in our schools for over 150 years. This transformation calls for a collective effort, moving beyond individual interests for the team's sake. It entails shifting our focus from "me" to "we," emphasizing collaboration on meaningful work. Sharing knowledge based on its impact on student learning is a highly valued skill. In my previous school, this was particularly crucial because we recognized that one teacher's effectiveness paled compared to the combined efforts of four, five, or six teachers engaged in the "right work."

In their book *Starting a Movement*, Ken Williams and Tom Hierck raise an essential question about school culture: Does it foster a competitive environment where teachers vie to be the best, comparing and ranking one another? Or does it thrive on collaboration, nurturing a collective commitment to improve for each other and our students?[87]

---

86. Mayo Clinic, "Mission and Values Statement on Teamwork," https://www.mayoclinic.org/about-mayo-clinic/mission-values.

87. Williams, Ken and Hierck, Tom, *Starting a Movement*, Solution Tree Press, 2015.

As an educator, will you proclaim, "Not on my watch, not on our watch, will this child not be successful"?

We should be willing to leverage the collective wisdom and expertise present in the room, utilizing all available knowledge, skills, and experiences to ensure that every child receives the same level of care and support we would provide to our children. I have personally witnessed the power of the team. When teams of educators genuinely believe in their ability to make a difference, they invariably do.

Collective Teacher Efficacy

In his research on educational effectiveness, John Hattie identified Collective Teacher Efficacy as having a significant impact with an effect size of 1.57. To put this into perspective, simply being alive as a student results in a growth of 0.10 standard deviations in one year. Being in an average teacher's classroom yields growth of 0.30 standard deviations. Therefore, being alive in the average teacher's classroom results in a growth of 0.40 standard deviations.

Collective Teacher Efficacy has almost four times the impact on student learning compared to an individual teacher. In their article "The Power of Collective Efficacy," Jenni Donohoo, John Hattie, and Rachel Eells affirm, "When teams of educators believe they have the ability to make a difference, exciting things can happen in a school."[88]

Team Defined

Before we proceed, we, as educators, must establish a shared understanding of the term "team." As a profession, we must ensure that key terms and acronyms are clearly defined and agreed upon. It is common for educators to use these terms loosely as if everyone has the same

---

88. Donohoo, Jenni, Hattie, John, and Eells, Rachel, "The Power of Collective Efficacy," *Educational Leadership*, March 2018.

understanding, and many times there is confusion. Therefore, let's take a moment to individually reflect and write our definitions of the word "team" below:

Write your definition of the word "team" in the space provided:

Here's a Story...
On This Teacher Team, All Has To Mean All... or Nobody Wins

By: Bob Eaker and Brian Butler, October 14, 2020

We were speaking to a team of teachers about their classrooms recently. This is what they described! **You won't want to miss this!**

During the planning meeting, the adult team talked about the lesson plan, identified essential skills that every student had to master, and talked about a consistent way that the adults would assess those essential skills. They looked over the video to evaluate the previous day's lesson. They took notes and talked about a plan for the entire team to get better, and then they looked at each student's strengths and areas where they needed additional time and targeted support, skill by skill, which would be addressed during the next lesson. Each adult in the room talked about their responsibility in working with all learners that the team of adults was responsible for but identified areas when the students broke into stations (rotations) where they would work on specific skills for each student.

All the adults were transparent regarding their strengths and openly shared areas where they felt uncomfortable teaching and demonstrating a particular skill. No problem, as their colleagues would show/model for them so they could learn to teach the skill better. For example, a coach who mainly played point guard (whom are we talking about friends) in college deferred to a coach who had extensive experience working with forwards and centers and would learn from that colleague.

As Bob shares in his presentation, **"Friday Night in America…A Commonsense Approach to Improve Student Achievement,"** *the Coaching Staff is a Collaborative Team. **The head coach cannot succeed alone, so they assemble a collaborative team of skilled professionals—the coaching staff."***

The team of coaches collectively created the practice (lesson) plan together. Each was comfortable using their coaching style during practice. The essential team goals during training would be worked on, but each player would be supported to work to improve their skills, whatever they were.

For example, the team goal of shooting 80% from the free throw line was not being met because a player consistently shot 60%. This player would shoot free throws with the entire team during the whole team portion of practice, then during stations, would spend two of the five skill stations working on free throws. One of the skill stations had three other players working with one coach, and one had the player working one-on-one with a coach who specialized in free throw shooting and was great and building relationships with players. They changed the ratio and the expertise of the individual instructing to make the practice/instruction more intense, exactly like is discussed in the book *Taking Action* as the authors share Response to Intervention at Work (RTI at Work) practices.[89]

---

89. Buffum, Austin, Mattos, Mike, and Malone, Janet, *Taking Action: A Handbook for RTI at Work*, Solution Tree Press, 2018.

After writing a plan for each player, the coaches were set for the next day's practice.

At the beginning of practice, the coaches addressed all players on the practice plan and what was ESSENTIAL for all players to know and be able to do over the next two hours. They modeled skills like chest pass, boxing out, correct shooting form, defensive stance, etc. They had the entire team practice together while coaches gave immediate feedback to those players so that they could observe needed corrections. The team goal for all players was to shoot 50% from the field and 80% from the free throw line in any drill, scrimmage, or set rotation throughout the practice. No matter who the player was, their goal was to meet this standard or bar of proficiency. For players who consistently meet or achieve beyond these shooting goals, the coaches with the player and coach set a realistic goal for that player and a timeline to achieve it. If a player was already an 85% free throw shooter, they might have set a goal of 90%, etc.

During practice, the coaches broke the players up into stations and rotated through different stations depending on the skills that needed more work. All players received instruction in the essential skills, but some players received more targeted time and support at certain stations because they were experiencing more difficulty with specific basketball skills. On top of that, some players were pulled to have even more targeted work one on one with a coach. In essence, they got what all players received plus they received two additional small group intensive sessions on skills they were yet to meet proficiency or expectations.

Also, throughout practice, which was videotaped, coaches gave constant feedback to players and took notes to reflect on later to prepare for the next practice session. This also would help them reflect on their coaching/teaching, which they would talk to each other about to enhance this continuous improvement cycle!

Another thing was expected throughout practice: every player was pushed a little out of their comfort zone for proper growth. It was also expected that an air of positivity and support would be present, with players supporting and encouraging each other to improve. The word *can't* was never used. The language "keep at it, you are not there yet" was heavily used throughout. But with passion, appropriate practice on the targeted skills, and persistence, all would master the skills. All did not get there at the same time or progress at the same rate, but the Bar, as Ken Williams and Tom Hierck assert in their book *Starting a Movement*, was the Bar for all.[90]

The positive culture of this group of coaches/teachers was framed by their unwavering belief in the ability of every Player/Student that they could achieve and perform at high levels, and it was their job to make it happen for every player. This team was heavily influenced by reading the book *Time for Change* by Anthony Muhammad and Luis Cruz.[91] Instead of looking out the window and hoping for better players, they said the players are the ones we have, and we have to get them there. Their motto, taken from a great educator Lillie Jessie, was "Mirror Check, Baby!"

The goal, as Bob shares in his breakout session **Friday Night In America**, for the coaching staff/collaborative team, is to create many winners on the team and prepare them for success not just on the court but in life. Bob says, "*Successful coaches set high expectations for their players—for their teams. Their goal is to ensure that all players perform at the highest levels.*" The culture of positive recognition and celebration was also evident during practice from player to player and coach to player, and even player to coach! This was like fuel for the engine of the team.

---

90. Williams, Ken and Hierck, Tom, *Starting a Movement*, Solution Tree Press, 2015.

91. Muhammad, Anthony and Cruz, Luis, *Time for Change: Four Essential Skills for Transformational School and District Leaders*, Solution Tree Press, 2019.

In the beginning, we would bet that most of you thought this was a school team, most likely in elementary school, because it described a workshop lesson model format with the whole group and then station or center rotations.

What do you think now?

Do these questions sound familiar?

1. What do we expect our students/players to know and be able to do?

2. How will we know if they have learned it (mastered the skill)?

3. How will we respond when they have not learned it?

4. How will we extend the learning for those who are already proficient?

They are the four critical questions of learning in the Professional Learning Communities at Work model. If you reread what we just wrote, you can align each question to how the coaches approached the learning for each player.

Have you visited a sports team of coaches recently? They are some of the best teachers in the world![92]

The previous narrative mirrors excellent teacher teams who, like skilled coaches, recognize that every student has gifts deserving of tailored experiences. Just as coaches assemble a collaborative team to guide athletes, teacher teams should unite with a shared belief and purpose, nurturing each student's unique strengths, passions, and talents. Just as athletes on the court, students are given the opportunity to reach new

---

92. Eaker, Bob and Butler, Brian, "On This Teacher Team, All Has To Mean All…or Nobody Wins," Solution Tree, https://www.solutiontree.com/blog/on-this-teacher-team-all-has-to-mean-all-or-nobody-wins/.

heights and push to beyond whatever they thought they were capable of accomplishing.

Defining *team* as we move forward in this book:

> *"A team is a group of individuals whose members work interdependently to achieve common goals for which members are mutually accountable."*
> —RICHARD DUFOUR, ET AL, *LEARNING BY DOING*[93]

Now that we have the definition of a team, let's unpack the definition even more. Take a moment to write your definition or understanding of the following keywords from the definition of the word *team* provided above.

Interdependently:

Common goals:

Mutually accountable:

---

93. DuFour, Richard, et al., *Learning by Doing: A Handbook for Professional Learning Communities at Work* (3rd ed.), Solution Tree Press, p. 12.

The most potent structure that supports student learning is one in which a team of educators teaches the same course or grade level. However, the ultimate message to any person fostering collective teacher efficacy is that everyone in the school should be a part of a team. Even if a teacher is the only one teaching that grade level or course, there are team structures that allow them to collaborate. Sometimes that may require creative solutions and structures, like electronic teams and logical-links teams, but in all cases, collaboration is essential for promoting collective teacher efficacy.

Various team structures facilitate meaningful collaboration. By employing these team structures, educators can foster effective collaboration, promote knowledge sharing, and ultimately enhance student learning outcomes.[94]

How similar are your definitions of the three key terms within the word *team* as defined below in Merriam-Webster Online Dictionary?

Interdependently:
the state of being dependent upon one another: mutual dependence

Common goals:
the end toward which effort is directed

Mutually accountable:
having a shared obligation or willingness to accept responsibility or to account for one's actions[95]

---

94. DuFour, Richard, et al., *Learning by Doing: A Handbook for Professional Learning Communities at Work* (3rd ed.), Solution Tree Press, p. 60-61.

95. https://www.merriam-webster.com/dictionary/

Having completed the reading of "On This Teacher Team, All Has To Mean All...or Nobody Wins" and considering the definition of the word *team* provided by DuFour et al., please identify instances in the story where you observed a focus on the following elements:

1. Interdependence

2. Common goals

3. Mutual accountability

List the specific parts of the story where you noticed these aspects being emphasized. This exercise will help you reflect on and recognize the presence of these important components within the context of your learning.

Consider the following quotes:

"The strength of the team is each individual member.
The strength of each member is the team."
—Phil Jackson[96]

"I am a member of the team, and I rely on the team, I defer to it
and sacrifice for it, because the team, not the individual,
is the ultimate champion."
—Mia Hamm[97]

"With an enthusiastic team, you can achieve
almost anything."
—Tahir Shah[98]

"You don't treat the so-called little people poorly, because we
don't have any little people here! The trainers, the managers, the
secretaries, the people who work in the dorms and cafeterias and
classroom buildings are all professionals,
and they're all important..."
—Bo Schembechler[99]

---

96. Wyatt, Christy, "What Phil Jackson's Leadership Teaches Us About Remote Team-Building," Entrepreneur, May 3, 2021, https://www.entrepreneur.com/leadership/what-phil-jacksons-leadership-teaches-us-about-remote/369620#:~:text=%22The%20strength%20of%20the%20team,would%20be%20collaborating%20over%20computers.

97. "Mia Hamm Quotes To Inspire and Motivate," Jobs in Football, May 8, 2022, https://jobsinfootball.com/blog/mia-hamm-quotes/ on August 2, 2023.

98. "Tahir Shah Quotes," AZ Quotes, https://www.azquotes.com/author/19333-Tahir_Shah.

99. "Bo Schembechler," Goodreads, https://www.goodreads.com/quotes/712391-you-don-t-treat-the-so-called-little-people-poorly-because-we.

Our Award Winning Custodial Team!

Mason Crest's Award-Winning Custodial Team

At Mason Crest, our custodial team demonstrated an incredible ability to embrace interdependence, working together toward common goals with mutual accountability. This outstanding teamwork led them to receive the prestigious award for the best custodial team in our region. Moreover, their dedication didn't stop there. They generously shared their knowledge and expertise, providing tutorials to the principal's team on the machines they used to maintain the building and grounds impeccably. Through their actions, the custodial team's leadership set a prime example for the entire staff, exemplifying the true spirit of teamwork at Mason Crest.

In the space below, write the story of a time when you were on a team that exhibited:

Interdependence

Common goals

Mutual accountability

Conversely, in the space below, write the story of a time when you were on a team that did *not* exhibit:

Interdependence

Common goals

Mutual accountability

Why were those two experiences so vastly different from one another?

Let's look at another variation of a team that embraced the following qualities:

Interdependence

Common goals

Mutual accountability

What Is Socratic Seminar?

STACEY DUFF EXPLAINS

During a Parent Teacher Organization (PTO) meeting in 2013, Stacey Duff, one of our reading teachers at Mason Crest, shared an insightful perspective. She shed light on the school's forward-thinking strategy to make advanced academic experiences available to a broader range of students in grades three to five. Traditionally, these opportunities were only given to students labeled as "gifted." However, a new approach was taking shape.

Duff explained the innovative use of Socratic seminars, a teaching method rooted in the ideas of Socrates. These seminars provided a platform for thoughtful discussions where students engaged with different types of written material like poems, nonfiction articles, and stories. After forming their individual responses to thought-provoking questions, students gathered in a circle to discuss using specific language like "I agree with," "I disagree with," and "I want to add on."

This approach aimed for inclusivity, allowing every student to share their thoughts and participate in meaningful conversations, no matter their previous labels. The main goal was to develop critical thinking skills and create an environment where students engaged deeply with the content. By incorporating multiple rounds of these seminars throughout the year, Mason Crest demonstrated a solid commitment to nurturing well-rounded intellectual growth and providing equal opportunities for enrichment.

In essence, Duff's explanation highlighted a modern shift away from traditional practices, showcasing a deliberate move toward ensuring that advanced academic resources were accessible to all students, encouraging each to reach higher levels of cognitive performance.[100]

Planning Socratic Seminar Collective Teacher Efficacy at Mason Crest Elementary School

POSTED ON BRIANBUTLER.INFO

The following blog was written to help capture the essence of how important the different teachers on this fourth-grade team were to the success of all students in benefiting from Socratic Seminar, an experience traditionally reserved for students with the gifted label.

To ensure that all students across the fourth grade were provided access to the Socratic Seminar, there had to be a 360-degree view of each student and the entire process.

This meant that not only the classroom teachers had to be involved in the plan, but the other teachers, such as the English

---

100. Duff, Stacey, Mason Crest Parent Teacher Organization (PTO) Meeting—Socratic Seminar Explanation, personal video, August 13, 2013.

Language Teacher, Special Education Teacher, and Advanced Academics Resource Teacher (AART), needed to be at the table sharing their unique knowledge, skills, expertise, and experiences. I asked a few of my former teachers to answer questions about the process of providing access to all students. You will notice that students were given targeted support, and we weren't just throwing them into the Socratic Seminar sink or swim. And most importantly, we were not dumbing the curriculum down as the grade level expectations were for all students.

Again, consider the word *team* and the critical components Interdependence, Common Goals, and Mutual Accountability as you read the blog "Planning Socratic Seminar Collective Teacher Efficacy at Mason Crest Elementary School" from brianbutler.info.

"When a team of individuals share the belief that through their unified efforts, they can overcome challenges and produce intended results, groups *are* more effective. For example, in schools, when educators believe in their combined ability to influence student outcomes, there are significantly higher levels of academic achievement (Bandura, 1993)."[101]

In working on my new workshop above, I reached out to several of my former colleagues from 2016 DuFour Award Recipient, Mason Crest Elementary School. At the end of the workshop my goal is to paint a picture of what it looks like for a team to ensure **relevant, differentiated, scaffolded and targeted access** to Socratic Seminar for each and every student (ALL)! I was not surprised by the responses I received, and it made me a bit nostalgic as I reminisced being a part of a school that created this haven for high levels of learning for every single student.

---

101. Bandura, Albert, "Perceived self-efficacy in cognitive development and functioning." *Educational Psychologist*, 28(2), 1993, 117-148.

Below are excerpts of the email responses I received from classroom teachers (Eric Burrell & Liz Scheurer), English Language Teacher (Kimberley Mathews) and Special Education Teacher (Laura Waggoner) who threw out their titles but shared their knowledge, skills, experience, and expertise to enhance the collective wisdom of the team. My question to them is first and then their answers:

Brian's Question:

How did you decide with your team when to do a Socratic Seminar? Was it tied to a certain standard or unit, or subject? As a part of the workshop, I want to have teams use the Socratic Seminar to engage in the experience of planning for all learners. Still, I wanted to know from start to finish how it was decided, including how you co-planned and taught background knowledge and pre-taught vocabulary, etc. to ensure all students had access.

Liz Scheurer—Classroom Teacher

I remember our team choosing to do one around Sonya Sotomayor because she was a great example of perseverance and how working hard can help you to reach your goals. Given the large Hispanic population at Mason Crest, I think we also thought she was a great role model as the first Hispanic Supreme Court Justice.

Additionally, we wanted to develop discourse. At the time, we were doing a great job as a team with supporting oral language with sentence frames for our English Language Learners (I think we were doing something called quality talk?) but we wanted to add in some opportunities for students to have meaningful conversations. Socratic seminars are great for getting students to have a position and support it, pushes them to elaborate and clarify, and synthesize all the ideas that are getting thrown at them.

Eric Burrell—Classroom Teacher

Liz's response to the Sonia Sotomayor Seminar was spot on. At one point Kimberley was pulling a group of English Language learners and providing some background knowledge and an additional text (I think) to help all students have access. The buildup and formal discussion of the Socratic Seminar directly correlates to the Fairfax County Public School (FCPS) standard "Demonstrates Active Listening Skills" (Citizenship Skill) as well as "Listens and speaks for specific purposes" (Language Arts skill).

Later, when I was still teaching 4th grade, I created a seminar based on the theme of sportsmanship. It seemed that 4th grade became a year where some of the competitiveness at recess was leading to some emotional outbursts that would carry back into the classroom and hinder the learning of some students during the afternoon. I also started putting together multiple resources (speeches, photos, videos) for students to synthesize as part of the seminar preparation. So instead of completing the general "Seminar Packet," I created a document that specifically addressed these various resources.

So, the following school year, in 5th grade, we used this seminar to discuss "Growth Mindset" and the idea of "Failing Up"... again this preparation involved reading an article, listening to a podcast (with pictures showcasing some of the ideas from the podcast), and exploring a Google Site (Nick Polak had made). Both the sportsmanship and "Failing Up" seminars were done within the first quarter as lessons for the students to carry out throughout the school year.

There are some more seminars that were directly connected to the content that we were teaching at the time. We used "The Blue Between" poem for a discussion during our poetry unit and "Was the Code of Hammurabi Just or Unjust?" after teaching Mesopotamia.

Kimberley Mathews—English Language Teacher (EL or ESOL)

The Advanced Academics Resource Teacher (AART) Morgan Huynh would suggest that we do a seminar and share some ideas. At that point, a member of the team would build on that idea or share another idea that was more directly related to the curriculum content or a situation that our students were facing (like not playing nice on the playground). From there, we would brainstorm the resources students could use to develop the background knowledge and critical questions. We would choose articles at different Lexile levels for multiple access points, read-aloud picture books, video clips, shared readings, etc. At that point, the ESOL Teacher (English Language Learners Teacher) and Special Education teachers would create materials that contained simplified language, sentence starters, word banks with important vocabulary, and other scaffolds and supports for the documents students would use to prepare for the seminar.

We've all heard this before, but we would then realize that what was good for English Language Learners was good for all and often use those materials for everyone. For instance, the book about Sotomayor was chosen for English Language Learners in mind because it offered picture support, and pages were both in Spanish and English. Laura and I pulled a group of students to read the book separately from the rest of the class— but to Liz's point, in later lessons, we used that book instead of the one-page article for the entire class because it was more engaging. In addition, it brought our students closer together as a class community because native English-speaking peers were in real time observing their Spanish only speaking peers have access to the content and interacting with it—everyone having connections together. It was a beautiful thing.

With this learning happening together, students were more willing to take a risk during the discussion part of the seminar and participate and others were more willing to give the needed wait time for their peer to explain their thinking. The real magic of a seminar is the discussion when students are listening to each other, having that meaningful conversation, but also being emotionally and cognitively connected to the learning and the opinions they have developed over the course of the seminar preparation. I love co-teaching and running a seminar with a new teacher that has never done it before. I hear comments like, "What if no one talks?" "What if students don't get it?" "This seems really silly moving the desks," but afterward they are always floored and amazed that ALL students could reach such high levels of learning.

The only way to make good on the promise of "ALL" is to create teams of teachers who take collective responsibility for each other's learning as teacher teammates and the learning of the students![102]

Think about the reading from this chapter and a team that you are presently on and answer the following reflection questions for teacher teams based on the words "interdependence," "common goals," and "mutual accountability":

Interdependence:

1. How have we actively supported and relied on one another as a team to enhance student learning?

2. What examples can we share where we have demonstrated interdependence by pooling our strengths and expertise?

102. Butler, Brian and contributors Scheurer, L., Burrell, E., Mathews, K., "Planning Socratic Seminar—Collective Teacher Efficacy at Mason Crest Elementary School," 2021, brianbutler.info.

3. In what ways have we fostered a collaborative environment where everyone feels valued and connected?

Common Goals:

1. Are our team goals clearly defined and aligned with our school's vision and mission?

2. How have we worked together to establish a shared understanding of our common goals?

3. What strategies have we used to ensure that our individual efforts contribute to our collective goals?

Mutual Accountability:

1. How have we held ourselves and each other accountable for meeting our agreed-upon expectations and commitments?

2. What steps have we taken to create a culture of open and honest feedback within our team?

3. In what ways have we celebrated our collective successes and addressed challenges together as a team?

These reflection questions can help teacher teams delve deeper into their collaborative practices and enhance their understanding and application of interdependence, common goals, and mutual accountability.

> "In schools with strong collective teacher efficacy, students learn more and their academic achievement increases. More than any other factor influencing student outcomes—for example, socioeconomic status, parent involvement, motivation, home environment, and concentration—collective teacher efficacy

> *impacts student achievement the most. In other words, when teams of teachers truly and fully believe in their collective ability to improve the learning of their students, their students do better and learn more."*
>
> —Gradecam[103]

Our Team Is a Hot Mess—Where Do We Begin?

I understand you may have doubts about the teams I described earlier. You're probably wondering how those high-performing teams reached that point, especially since the teams you work with struggle to agree. You all have trouble playing nicely and being comfortable enough to be vulnerable with each other. Instead, you tend to work alongside each other without truly collaborating. You're looking for tools to help your team function better, where interdependence, common goals, and mutual accountability are the norm.

These are excellent questions and thoughts. It's important to know that different teams develop at different rates and go through various stages in their journey. Understanding these stages and reflecting on your current situation is crucial to progress. In the groundbreaking 2002 book *The Five Dysfunctions of a Team*, author Patrick Lencioni describes the common challenges teams face as they try to "grow together."

Lencioni identifies the first dysfunction of a team as the ***absence of trust***. This occurs when team members are uncomfortable being vulnerable, open, and honest with each other. Without trust, team members become *afraid of conflict*. However, healthy and productive conflict around ideas is essential for a team's growth. When there's a ***fear of conflict***, it leads to a ***lack of commitment***. People may not fully commit to the team's goals or processes because they haven't engaged in healthy and productive conflicts about ideas.

103. "What is Collective Teacher Efficacy (CTE)?" Gradecam, June 20, 2020, https://gradecam.com/2020/07/what-is-collective-teacher-efficacy-cte/.

The fourth dysfunction of a team is the ***unwillingness to hold one another accountable***. High-performing teams hold each other accountable. Remembering the definition of a team and the concept of mutual accountability is essential. Lencioni explains it's a peer-to-peer responsibility because team members have committed to decisions through healthy conflicts and trust. They willingly confront each other and hold one another accountable for what's necessary to ensure the team's success. Finally, the fifth dysfunction of a team is ***inattention to results***. In other words, a team is not truly a team without a common goal and a focus on achieving results. Without a goal, it's just a group working together without a clear purpose.[104]

Almost sixty years ago, Bruce Tuckman identified the stages of development that teams move through. High-performing teams typically go through several stages of development as they grow and mature. Here is a list of typical stages that teams often experience:

1. Forming: This is the initial stage where team members come together and get to know each other. Roles and responsibilities are established, and there is a sense of excitement and anticipation about the team's goals.

2. Storming: In this stage, conflicts and disagreements may arise as team members assert their ideas and opinions. There can be power struggles or differences in approaches, which need to be addressed and resolved for the team to progress.

3. Norming: During this stage, the team establishes norms, values, and a set of agreed-upon behaviors. Team members better understand each other's strengths and weaknesses, and cooperation and collaboration become more prevalent.

---

104. Lencioni, Patrick M., *The Five Dysfunctions of a Team*, Jossey-Bass, 2002.

4. Performing: At this stage, the team has achieved a high level of trust, collaboration, and efficiency. They work seamlessly together toward shared goals, leveraging individual strengths and supporting each other's growth. The team is self-directed and can handle challenges effectively.

5. Adjourning: In some cases, teams may reach a stage where their mission or project comes to an end. Adjourning involves wrapping up the work, celebrating achievements, and acknowledging the contributions of team members. This stage allows for reflection and learning before team members move on to new projects or teams.[105]

In conclusion, grasping the trajectory of team development outlined by Patrick Lencioni and Bruce Tuckman offers invaluable insights into nurturing collaboration and cultivating each student's unique strengths, passions, and talents. Teacher teams committed to providing gifted experiences to all students, regardless of labels, can similarly advance through stages as they build trust, engage in constructive conflicts, and establish norms, ultimately working cohesively toward shared objectives. By embracing the principles of interdependence, mutual accountability, and a focus on outcomes, educators can guide their teams through these developmental phases, enabling them to unlock each student's unlimited potential and thrive as a united and accomplished cohort in this continuous improvement journey.

---

105. Tuckman, B. W., "Developmental sequence in small groups," *Psychological Bulletin*, 63(6), 1965, pp. 384-399.

Helpful Team Tools

TEAM NORMS—WHY?

Here's a Story...
A High School English Department Discusses Team Norms

In the English department office at Anywhere High School, a group of teachers gathered for a meeting before the start of the school year. They discussed the importance of team norms in creating a positive and collaborative work environment.

An experienced English teacher, **Alison**, raised her hand to get everyone's attention. "Let's talk about team norms and why they matter," she said.

Jaivon, a new teacher, asked, "Why are team norms so important? Can't we rely on our skills?"

Alison smiled and replied, "We're all talented educators, but team norms serve a bigger purpose. They help us understand how we'll work together, communicate effectively, and support each other. Norms ensure that everyone's voice is heard and respected."

Emily, another experienced teacher, added, "Exactly! Norms provide clear expectations for how we interact. They help us handle disagreements, solve problems together, and build trust. Without norms, we risk misunderstandings, conflicts, and inefficiencies."

Kathleen, known for her thoughtful insights, said, "Team norms also make us accountable to each other and our students. When we commit to specific norms, we hold ourselves and each other responsible. This leads to consistency and reliability in our teaching practices."

As the conversation continued, teachers shared stories of how team norms had made a positive impact. **Emily** talked about how their norm of open communication and constructive feedback transformed their lesson-planning sessions into opportunities for growth and innovation.

Inspired by the stories, **Jaivon** exclaimed, "I see how team norms can elevate our collective impact. They help us work toward common goals, maximize our strengths, and support each other's growth. Strong norms will make us a strong and united team."

The teachers agreed, and **Alison** concluded, "Developing team norms requires our active participation and commitment. Let's work together to define our unique set of norms for the English team. This will create an environment where each of us can thrive. Together, we'll make a remarkable difference in our students' lives."

The teachers left the room feeling motivated and unified as the meeting ended. They understood the importance of team norms and were determined to develop and embrace them. They knew that by doing so, they would create a collaborative and empowering space where teachers and students could flourish.

Team Norms—Here's What

Team norms are agreed-upon commitments that govern the behavior and interactions of team members. They serve as a framework for how team members should engage with one another, make decisions, and work toward common goals. Team norms establish a shared understanding of expected behaviors and promote a positive and productive team culture.

These norms can cover various aspects, such as communication, participation, respect, and problem-solving. They help foster trust, collaboration, and accountability within the team, ensuring everyone is on the same page and working together effectively. Norms provide clarity, promote consistency, and contribute to the overall success and cohesion of the team.

1. Communication Norms: These are the established guidelines for how team members communicate with one another. They may include active listening, respectful and constructive feedback, clarity in expressing ideas, and timely response to messages.

2. Participation Norms: These norms determine the expected level of engagement and involvement from each team member. They outline the importance of active participation, sharing ideas, and contributing to discussions and decision-making processes.

3. Decision-Making Norms: These norms define the methods and processes used by the team to reach decisions. They may include seeking consensus, considering diverse perspectives, and allowing for open dialogue before finalizing choices.

4. Accountability Norms: These norms focus on individual and collective responsibility within the team. They establish the expectation that team members will fulfill their commitments, meet deadlines, and take ownership of their actions and outcomes.

5. Respect Norms: These norms promote a culture of respect and inclusivity within the team. They encourage treating one another with kindness, valuing diverse viewpoints, and creating a safe space for everyone to express their thoughts and opinions.

6. Confidentiality Norms: These norms address the importance of maintaining confidentiality and trust within the team. They outline the need to keep sensitive information shared within the team confidential, fostering an environment where members feel safe to share openly.

7. Conflict Resolution Norms: These norms provide guidance on how conflicts and disagreements should be addressed within the team. They emphasize the importance of resolving conflicts constructively, through open dialogue, active listening, and finding mutually beneficial solutions.

By establishing and adhering to team norms, members can create a positive and productive working environment that supports collaboration, effective communication, and shared goals.

There are many ways to go about creating norms for teams. The following is one way in which I have helped teams go about creating norms.

Team Norms—Here's How

Protocol for establishing team norms:

Brainstorming: Conduct a brainstorming session with team members to generate ideas for team norms. Encourage everyone to contribute their suggestions without judgment or criticism.

Identify Key Areas: Group the brainstormed ideas into critical areas or themes that reflect the team's needs and priorities—for example, communication, collaboration, participation, respect, decision-making, and time management.

Discussion and Consensus: Facilitate a discussion around each identified area and encourage team members to share their thoughts, concerns, and preferences. Seek consensus on the norms that should be established for each area.

Draft Norms: Based on the discussions, create a draft document that outlines the agreed-upon team norms. Ensure that each norm is clear, specific, and actionable. Use positive language to emphasize desired behaviors.

Review and Feedback: Share the draft norms with the team and provide an opportunity for feedback. Encourage team members to review the document carefully and suggest any necessary revisions or additions.

Consensus Building: Facilitate a consensus-building process to address any differences or concerns raised during the feedback stage. Encourage open and respectful dialogue to reach a shared understanding and agreement on the final set of team norms. DuFour et al. asserted that a group has arrived at consensus when two criteria have been met:

1. All points of view have not just merely been heard but have been actively solicited.

2. The will of the group is evident even to those who oppose it.[106]

One way of coming to consensus is by using the "Fist to Five" strategy.

The "Fist to Five" consensus is a decision-making strategy commonly used in team settings. It allows individuals to express their level of agreement or support for a proposed idea or course of action using hand signals on a scale from one to five.

Here's a breakdown of the scale:

- Fist: Represents complete disagreement or lack of support.

- One finger: Indicates minimal agreement or support.

- Two fingers: Suggests some agreement or support, but with reservations or concerns.

---

106. Dufour, Richard, et al., *Learning by Doing: A Handbook for Professional Learning Communities at Work* (3rd ed.), Solution Tree Press, p. 32.

- Three fingers: Represents moderate agreement or support.
- Four fingers: Indicates strong agreement or support.
- Five fingers: Represents complete agreement and strong support.

During a discussion or decision-making process, participants are asked to show their hand signals simultaneously, indicating their level of agreement or support. This visual representation allows the facilitator and team members to quickly gauge the consensus and identify any differences of opinion.

The purpose of the "Fist to Five" consensus is to encourage open communication, active participation, and shared decision-making within the group. It helps to surface differing viewpoints, facilitates discussion, and allows individuals to reconsider their positions based on the collective input.

By using this strategy, teams can work toward reaching a consensus by addressing concerns, exploring alternative options, and finding common ground. It promotes collaboration, ensures that everyone's voice is heard, and leads to more inclusive and effective decision-making processes.

Document Finalized Norms: Once consensus is reached, document the finalized team norms in a clear and accessible format. This could be a shared document or a poster displayed in a team meeting space for easy reference.

Commitment and Signatures: Ask each team member to demonstrate their commitment to the established norms by signing the document or expressing their written agreement. This symbolic gesture reinforces the importance of accountability.

Communication and Implementation: Share the finalized team norms with all team members and any relevant stakeholders. Discuss the norms in team meetings, orientations, or professional learning sessions to ensure everyone understands them.

Regular Review and Reflection: Review team norms at the beginning of each meeting to assess their effectiveness and relevance. Encourage team members to reflect on how well they are adhering to the norms and suggest any necessary adjustments or improvements.

By following this protocol, teams can collaboratively establish clear and agreed-upon norms that guide their interactions, promote a positive team culture, and contribute to their collective success.

Accountability Protocol

We have norms, and when they are not followed, we all look around to see who will hold the one violating the norm accountable. How will you hold each other accountable for the norms you developed and agreed upon? If you have taken the time to develop team norms but don't have a safe way of holding each other accountable, then you don't have team norms. This is a critical step!

Here's a Story...
Cheers! Here's to "Norm"

LAUGHTER AND LEVITY CAN DEFUSE DEFENSIVENESS,
BUT YOU MUST KNOW EACH OTHER AS TEAMMATES.

A team of dedicated teachers decided to implement an accountability protocol to address each other when arriving late to team meetings. Inspired by the memorable character Norm from the TV show *Cheers*, they came up with a creative and lighthearted solution involving a Norm cutout.

During their meeting, if a tardy colleague entered the room, they were greeted by the sight of a life-sized Norm cutout seated at the table, complete with a cup of coffee in hand. The team member often couldn't contain their amusement when using this protocol. The room filled with laughter, creating a lighthearted and positive atmosphere.

The Norm cutout became a symbol of accountability within the team. Whenever someone was late to a meeting, the Norm cutout would make its appearance, taking their place at the table. The team members found it to be an effective and enjoyable way to address the tardiness issue while fostering a sense of camaraderie and collective responsibility.

The Norm cutout served as a friendly reminder to uphold the agreed-upon norm of punctuality. It not only lightened the mood but also sparked conversations about the importance of respecting each other's time and the impact of tardiness on the team's productivity and cohesion.

Over time, the Norm cutout became an integral part of the team's meetings, and everyone embraced its presence as a humorous yet meaningful accountability tool. It helped create a supportive and respectful environment where team members felt motivated to be punctual and engaged during their collaborative sessions.

The teacher team's creative use of the Norm cutout not only addressed the issue of lateness but also strengthened their bonds and improved their overall team dynamics. It showcased the power of accountability protocols that combine humor, camaraderie, and a shared commitment to professional growth and collaboration.

Fourth Grade Team Norms	
Time • When do we meet? • Will we set a beginning and end time? • Will we start and end on time?	• We will start (10:20) and end (11:14) each meeting at the established time.
Listening • How will we encourage listening? • How will we discourage interrupting?	• We will be present and respectful in conversations, as active listeners.
Decision Making • How will we make decisions? • Are we an advisory or decision making body? • Will we reach decisions by consensus? • How will we deal with conflicts?	• We will be flexible in our decision making process to reach a group consensus and consider all viewpoints.
Participation • How will we encourage everyone's participation? • Will we have an attendance policy?	• We will invite and include all necessary logical links to our team meetings and communication. • We will review the agenda and prepare for upcoming topics *with* **questions** and **ideas** in mind. • We will share **responsibilities** (such as data collection.
Expectations • What do we expect from members? • Are there requirements for participation?	• We will be **positive** and we will make time to laugh each day. • We will work together and **share ideas**, lessons, and resources. • Our meetings will be **agenda** driven.

Accountability Protocol:

- Address violations *right away*. **Example**: In a *polite* voice state, "Hey, listen…that's a norm. Get with it." Or "What unites us?" (positive approach), "Here is my understanding of the situation…what's yours?"
- **Communicate** when you need more time to process the information/question.

Do We Know Each Other?
Do We Know Ourselves First?

"Without reflection, we go blindly on our way, creating more unintended consequences, and failing to achieve anything useful."
—MARGARET J. WHEATLEY[107]

Sometimes, despite the structures and protocols in place to support our teams, there are instances when team members still fail to connect. I experienced such a situation while working with my co-principal, Diane Kerr, at Mason Crest. A grade-level teacher team constantly seemed on different pages, so it became personal. Diane and I communicated on this section as we revisited this situation from our time together. Unsure of how to resolve the issue, we sought the help of Diane's husband, Gib, an expert in a specific type of inventory that examines thinking and behavior preferences.

We decided to have Gib administer this inventory to our teachers, as it is rooted in brain research and designed to enhance communication, teamwork, and workplace performance. The key aspect of this inventory is self-awareness and understanding others with different thinking and behavior preferences. It explores various ways we communicate and perceive ourselves, such as analytical, conceptual, structural, or social preferences. Typically, people lean toward two of these preferences. The inventory also highlights an individual's behavioral preferences, such as assertiveness, flexibility, and expressiveness. These behavior preferences impact perceptions.

When you have a specific thinking and behavior preference and operate based on it, those with different preferences may appear combative or constantly opposed to your ideas. This can lead to personal conflicts. Therefore, we asked this team if they would be amenable to taking this

---

107. Wheatley, Margaret, "It's an Interconnected World," http://margaretwheatley.com/articles/interconnected.html.

inventory. Before that, Diane and I took the inventory ourselves to set an example and to improve our collaboration as co-principals.

I emphasize this point because many arguments, disagreements, and frustrations within teams, even with established norms and protocols, require us to introspect. We must reflect on our contributions and understand how our thinking and behavior preferences may differ from others. Likewise, we should consider whether their thinking and behavior preferences differ from ours, making it difficult for us to comprehend their perspectives.

Helping this team gain self-understanding and comprehend each other was crucial for their progress. After taking the inventory and having Gib coach them through their preferences, the team members had a huge "aha" around the behavioral piece and how different their thinking preferences were. There was almost immediate change in the dynamics of the team.

Suppose you find yourself in a situation where you have established team norms, accountability protocols, and decision-making processes but are still facing obstacles. In that case, it is essential to acknowledge the personal dynamics at play. It's not a matter of good or bad; it's simply a reflection of who we are. Some individuals may be so fundamentally different that finding common ground becomes challenging unless they recognize their own and others' operating styles. This recognition fosters understanding, empathy, and compassion. Ultimately, it boils down to considering what we would want for our children. When we adopt that perspective, we become willing to examine ourselves and make improvements to benefit ourselves and our students.

As a reflection question, consider times when your teams have been provided with structures, protocols, and support yet still struggled to make progress. I intentionally didn't mention a specific inventory because several are available that encourage introspection and help us understand our thinking styles, personalities, and how they shape our worldview. By embracing these tools, we can gain a fresh perspective and comprehend that others may perceive the world differently, leading to better teamwork, mutual accountability, interdependence, and shared goals—all for the benefit of our students.

"Self-reflection is a humbling process. It's essential to find out why you think, say, and do certain things...then better yourself."

—SONYA TECLAI[108]

The Power of Collaboration and Collective Teacher Efficacy

In this chapter, we have explored the profound impact of collaboration and collective teacher efficacy in nurturing each student's unique strengths, passions, and talents. As we conclude this chapter, we are reminded of a powerful story that encapsulates the transformative nature of these principles and the collective responsibility we share as educators.

Here's a Story...
Based on True Events

Picture this: A student arrived at our school from another country where English was not their first language. Having experienced turmoil at their previous schools, the student carried a reputation for behavioral issues that deviated from the norm. As educators, we recognized the importance of providing a fresh start and embarked on a mission to ensure the student's success.

Driven by our commitment to collective teacher efficacy, we assembled a team of dedicated professionals. From administrators, to the grade level teacher team, to the counselor, to the physical education, the art teachers, the music, the English

108. "Sonya Teclai," Goodreads, https://www.goodreads.com/author/quotes/14203760.
Sonya_Teclai.

Language Teacher, and reading and mathematics specialist, we all understood that our collective effort was essential for the student's growth. We forged a comprehensive support system to address academic, social, and emotional needs.

Collaboration became our guiding principle. We delved into the student's background, learning about their likes, dislikes, and previous experiences. It became apparent that their negative outlook on education stemmed from feeling isolated and being unfamiliar with the expectations of a new country's schooling system. We recognized the need to bridge these gaps and create a tailored plan for their success.

Proactively, we engaged the counselor to provide ongoing support, conducted pre-assessments in literacy and math, and discovered the student's strength in mathematics. Building on this interest, we fostered a connection between the student and our music teacher, igniting a passion for drumming. We integrated their love for music into their education, offering individual drumming lessons and placing them in advanced math classes to both challenge and support their growth.

Though the journey was not without its hurdles, we remained steadfast in our belief in collective teacher efficacy. The team coordinated efforts, ensuring the student received the necessary academic, emotional, and behavioral support. We front-loaded language instruction, modeled appropriate behavior, and rallied around them, leaving no stone unturned.

Over time, the impact of our collaboration and collective responsibility became evident. The student blossomed, surpassing all expectations. Their family expressed immense gratitude for the support provided during those critical years. Today, the student thrives in high school, a testament to the power of collective teacher efficacy and our unwavering commitment to every student's unlimited potential.

As we conclude this chapter, we are reminded of the obligation we have as a team. By embracing collective teacher efficacy, we can break down barriers and create an educational environment where every student receives the support and opportunities they deserve. Let this story inspire us to continue fostering collaboration, collective responsibility, and the belief that every student deserves a gifted education.

Reflection Questions for Educators:

1. How does the story of collective teacher efficacy and collaboration resonate with your own experiences as an educator?

2. In what ways have you witnessed the power of collaboration in supporting students with diverse backgrounds and needs?

3. Reflecting on the vignette, how can you contribute to creating a culture of collective responsibility within your school or educational community?

These reflection questions are meant to encourage analysis of the reader's current practices, beliefs, and potential areas for growth in fostering collective teacher efficacy and collaboration. By engaging in thoughtful self-reflection, educators can further enhance their ability to support each student's strengths, passions, and talents.

Now that we have established the essential foundation in Chapters 1, 2, and 3, readers are now equipped with the knowledge and mindset to deeply engage with the subsequent chapters. Chapter 4, titled "O=Our Superpowers," takes the journey further by identifying seven powerful strategies for educators to become competent and confident individuals and teams to create a learning environment where each student's unique strengths, passions, and talents can be uncovered and nourished.

The second part of the chapter will focus on empowering students with their superpowers, exploring various attributes that contribute to overall well-being and success as we progress from the prep work of preparing the room to be painted (previous chapters). It is now time to paint the room in Chapters 4 and 5.

CHAPTER 4

O = Our Superpowers

"If you match up solid research and solid strategies, you will get results!"

—Eric Jensen[109]

Throughout my career, I've been fortunate to witness various educational approaches that educators employ, leading to students' benefits. Frequently, I found myself implementing approaches that felt right with my colleagues, even without being fully aware of the underlying research or able to identify the approach's name precisely. As I transitioned into an administrative role and became more of a student of various approaches, I was able to put a name to our methods.

Prominent figures like Gholdy Muhammad, Carol Ann Tomlinson, Yvette Jackson, and Zaretta Hammond have written and illuminated many approaches that align with my beliefs, and some of the strategies in this section have been adapted from their work.[110] They and others have also significantly shaped my perspective on ways to nurture each student's unique strengths, passions, and talents.

In this chapter, we will explore how teacher teams can apply these

---

109. Jensen, Eric, *Teaching with the Brain in Mind*, ASCD, 2005.

110. Muhammad, Gholdy, *Cultivating Genius: An Equity Framework for Culturally and Historically Responsive Literacy*, Scholastic, 2020. Tomlinson, Carol Ann and Javius, Edwin Lou, "For Each to Excel: Teach Up for Excellence," *Educational Leadership*, 69(5), February 1, 2012, 28-33, https://www.ascd.org/el/articles/teach-up-for-excellence. Jackson, Yvette and Feuerstein, Reuven, *The Pedagogy of Confidence Inspiring High Intellectual Performance in Urban Schools*, Teachers College Press, 2011. Hammond, Zaretta, *Ready for Rigor: A Framework for Culturally Responsive Teaching*, 2013.

strategies to unlock the unlimited potential of their students. While it is not an exhaustive list of strategies, as there are many other strategies educators might find effective and should continue to use, I have included the ones that significantly impact learning based on my experience and learning as an educator. Coupling solid research with these strategies can have a high likelihood of yielding impactful results.

Teacher Superpowers—Seven Powerful Strategies

1. Harvesting Student Strengths and Centering Student Perspectives

2. Fostering Connections and Connecting Learning: Empowering Students Through Relationships and Relevance

3. Elevating High Cognitive Performance

4. Offering Enhanced Learning Experiences

5. Identifying Prerequisites to Ensure Learning

6. Acknowledging Different Points of Entry into the Curriculum

7. Creating a Flexible Classroom

Harvesting Student Strengths and Centering Perspectives

"Strength-Based Learning isn't about weaknesses. It's about building the confidence of learners so they can see their unique gifts and build on those areas that are challenging without the notion that they aren't smart or good enough based on the one size fits all approach."

—PENNY MEYER, 2003[111]

---

111. Meyer, Penny, "Strength-Based Education, LinkedIn, March 5, 2003, https://www.linkedin.com/pulse/strengths-based-education-penny-meyer.

Here's a Story...
Doris and Paul Butler Sr. Elementary School

At Doris and Paul Butler Sr. Elementary School, all staff members were committed to creating high-performing teams at each grade level. At this school, the mantra was "Our expectations and beliefs create a world of endless possibilities for students!" Here is an example of that mantra being lived out with this one team.

Mr. Cunningham, Ms. Isiah, and Mr. Ausbrooks were passionate educators who believed in the power of harvesting and activating student strengths. They knew each child possessed unlimited potential and unique talents waiting to be discovered.

As the school year began, the teacher team embarked on a mission to uncover their students' strengths. They met regularly to share insights, observations, and strategies. During these team meetings, they discussed student work samples, anecdotal records, and assessments to understand each child better.

One day, as the team reviewed student portfolios, they noticed a recurring theme—artistic flair. They marveled at the imaginative drawings, colorful paintings, and intricate crafts. The team recognized the unlimited potential of their students' artistic abilities and saw an opportunity to ignite their passion further.

With their combined expertise, Mr. Cunningham, Ms. Isiah, and Mr. Ausbrooks crafted a plan to activate the students' artistic strengths. They sought the collaboration of the school's art teachers, Mrs. Lopez and Mr. Ramirez, who were thrilled to support the team's vision.

The teacher team and the art teachers began by integrating art across the curriculum. They incorporated visual representations and geometric designs in math, allowing students to explore concepts creatively. The art teachers shared their expertise in using art to enhance mathematical understanding, helping students visualize abstract concepts through drawings and manipulatives.

In language arts, the team and the art teachers encouraged students to illustrate stories and create their own picture books. The art teachers provided guidance on composition, color theory, and different artistic styles, helping students bring their narratives to life visually. This collaborative effort enriched the language arts curriculum and provided students with a platform to showcase their creativity.

To foster a supportive environment, the team and the art teachers established an "Artistic Showcase" in the school's hallway. Students' artwork adorned the walls, displaying their unique talents for the entire school community to admire. They also organized weekly "Artist Spotlight" sessions, where students could share their creative process and inspire their peers.

Furthermore, the teacher team collaborated with local artists, inviting them as guest speakers and conducting workshops. These interactions exposed students to different art forms and allowed them to learn from professionals in the field. The art teachers played a vital role in coordinating these opportunities, connecting the team with artists who could provide valuable insights and inspire the students' artistic pursuits.

As the weeks went by, the students' confidence soared. Their artwork became more sophisticated, and they began expressing themselves in ways they never had before. Students who once felt reserved or struggled academically found solace and a sense of accomplishment through their artistic pursuits.

The teacher team harvested a world of strengths, unlocking the unlimited potential within their students. Through their collaboration with the art teachers, they harvested and cultivated the artistic talents of their students, fostering a supportive and inspiring environment.

In an entire staff learning session about strengths, the team shared their experience with the other teams. Doris and Paul Butler Sr. Elementary School encouraged and expected all staff members to share, fostering a culture of collaboration and continuous improvement. Their story, including the collaboration with the art teachers, served as a shining example of the school's commitment to teamwork and recognizing the unlimited potential of both students and educators.

At Doris and Paul Butler Sr. Elementary School, the belief in the power of collaboration and shared expertise was woven into the fabric of the school culture. The teacher team's collaboration with the art teachers enhanced the students' artistic abilities and created a supportive and inspiring environment for all. The school truly embodied the Mayo Clinic's value of teamwork, valuing all contributions and blending individual staff members' skills in unsurpassed collaboration.

Harvesting Strengths—A Conversation with Author Katie White

During the podcast "A Conversation With Brian," author Katie White shared a compelling story about a fourth-grade team she worked with, highlighting the profound impact of starting with strengths.[112] The team embarked on a writing task with their students, collecting their samples and placing them in the center of the table. Instead of focusing on weaknesses, they embarked on a process Katie referred to as "harvesting" strengths, inspired by the work of Fullan and Dam.

In a brainstorming session, the team established success criteria and goals for their students. They then analyzed the students' work but

---

112. Katie White—Author & Assessment Expert," A Conversation With Brian (podcast), January 26, 2022, http://media.rss.com/aconversationwithbriannardosking17/feed.xml.

with a unique perspective. Their purpose was not to score or identify errors but to recognize and appreciate each student's strengths. Katie encouraged the team to jot down one to three strengths they noticed on sticky notes, allowing them to immerse themselves in this positive approach fully.

As the team diligently carried out the exercise, a seasoned teacher had a revelation. She genuinely expressed surprise that she had never looked at student work solely for their strengths. The realization filled her with optimism, a sense that she could make a difference. This powerful revelation sparked an enthusiastic discussion about the consequences of solely focusing on gaps and how it restricts our ability to see the unlimited potential in our students.

Continuing their journey of harvesting strengths, the team took a remarkable step the following day. Equipped with the writing samples, the teachers meticulously documented every strength they had observed in the students' work. When the students arrived, their assessments were returned without any written comments. Instead, they were instructed to partner up and review their work and that of their peers. The task was to identify the strengths that belonged to each student.

This transformative exercise empowered the students to recognize and acknowledge their strengths, fostering a sense of celebration and pride. Every student possessed at least one strength, instilling in them a profound sense of self-worth. The process allowed the students to set specific goals based on their identified strengths, guiding their subsequent attempts. Areas that didn't align with their strengths or represented skills yet to be developed became their goals.

The impact on the classroom atmosphere was nothing short of remarkable. Students felt valued and motivated, embracing their strengths and working toward their goals. As the teacher described, the transformative power of starting with strengths cannot be overstated.

Katie passionately implored all teachers to adopt this approach, recognizing its immense benefits for teachers and students. By beginning with strengths, teachers can create an environment where students feel seen, valued, and inspired to activate their unlimited potential. It is a practice that has the power to make a profound difference in the lives of both educators and students alike.

Teacher teams have the superpower to identify and activate each student's unique strengths and empower students to use their perspectives and voices in various ways. By recognizing their talents, interests, and abilities, teacher teams can tailor instruction to engage and inspire students.

Other Examples:

In a team of math teachers, one might identify a student's talent for problem-solving and assign them leadership roles in group activities. In contrast, another teacher might recognize students' artistic abilities and incorporate visual representations into their lessons to enhance understanding.

Empowering students as active participants in their education: A music teacher-team might involve students in selecting the repertoire for a concert, allowing them to have a say in their musical experiences.

Thought Spark Questions: Harvesting Student Strengths and Centering Student Perspectives

1. How can we shift our focus from weaknesses to recognizing and harvesting students' strengths?

2. What strategies can we employ to create a supportive and inspiring environment for students to showcase their unique talents and abilities?

3. How can collaboration with other teachers or specialists help activate and nurture students' strengths?

4. How can we empower students to recognize and appreciate their strengths?

5. In what ways can we involve students in decision-making and

utilize their perspectives and voices in their education?

6. What opportunities can we provide for students to share their strengths with their peers and the wider community?

7. How can we continuously improve our practice in identifying and activating students' strengths through collaboration with colleagues?

Fostering Connections and Connecting Learning

EMPOWERING STUDENTS THROUGH RELATIONSHIPS AND RELEVANCE

"Who we are cannot be separated from where we're from."

—MALCOLM GLADWELL[113]

Since I began my career as an educator, I've consistently heard from my colleagues that a positive teacher-student relationship is essential for meaningful and consistent learning in school and classroom settings. As discussed in Chapter 1, the brain's neurotransmitter oxytocin plays a crucial role in forming these positive relationships. Simply put, oxytocin assists the brain in establishing strong bonds of loyalty and trust, enabling individuals to cultivate significant connections with others.

In the book *Building Bridges*, Dr. Don Parker writes: "Beth K. Larkins-Strathy and Diana J. LaRocco (2007) discuss the effect that caring teachers have on prosocial behavior and academic achievement. They found that students achieve at higher levels when they are in educational environments characterized as caring. Making caring connections is a way that schools can provide high-quality education and produce high-achieving students. Students who perceive their teachers as caring

---

113. Gladwell, Malcolm, *Outliers*, Back Bay Books, 2009, p. 221.

have higher levels of motivation, effort, participation, and engagement... But what is caring? Students describe caring as creating an environment of respect, empathy, fairness, and acceptance, where they are free to make mistakes."[114]

During my podcast "A Conversation With Brian" (March 9, 2002), I had the opportunity to interview Dr. Parker. Our discussion centered on the significance of teacher-student relationships and their impact on student motivation. Don shared his insights, emphasizing the transformative power of positive connections between teachers and students.[115]

Don firmly believed that relationships, especially positive ones between students and teachers, played a crucial role in stimulating emotions and motivating students. According to him, when teachers establish strong relationships with their students, it creates a profound sense of connection and purpose. As a result, students become more motivated to learn because they value their relationship with their teacher. This mutual appreciation not only benefits the students but also the teachers themselves. It enables teachers to present the content in a way that resonates with students, making the learning experience more enjoyable and rewarding for everyone involved.

He emphasized the importance of building meaningful connections and understanding students' lives. By doing so, teachers can help students succeed academically by mastering the content and contributing to their overall success in life. Don pointed out that students often view their teachers as role models. When students feel comfortable opening up and sharing their personal experiences, it becomes easier for teachers to guide and support them. He emphasized that students genuinely appreciate when teachers show interest in their personal lives, rather than solely focusing on their academic achievements.

Don further shared an intriguing perspective based on research. When affluent students were asked about the type of teacher they needed

114. Parker, Don, *Building Bridges*, Solution Tree Press, 2019.

115. Brian Butler, "A Conversation with Brian," March 9, 2002, Episode 5, YouTube, https://youtu.be/3mGA-xKSD98.

to succeed, they emphasized the importance of being pushed to excel and prepare for higher education and careers. However, students from lower socioeconomic backgrounds or middle-class families responded differently. They expressed a strong need for teachers who genuinely cared about them. This insight highlighted the significance of building strong relationships to effectively support students from diverse backgrounds.

Don's perspective emphasized the transformative power of teacher-student relationships. By fostering positive connections, teachers can inspire and motivate students, leading them toward academic success and helping them thrive in their personal lives. Building these relationships and understanding students' lives are vital components of effective teaching and profoundly impact students' motivation and well-being.

Fostering Connections and Empowering Students: Insights from Greg Taylor, an Experienced Teacher

Greg Taylor, a fantastic teacher with over thirty years of experience, shared his wisdom from the 2022-23 school year regarding the superpower of Fostering Connections and Connecting Learning: Empowering Students Through Relationships and Relevance. Here is what Greg had to say:

> This year has been quite a journey for me. Due to a severe shortage of teachers, I was reassigned from my role as a mentor teacher in the central office to a classroom position at a high vacancy school. Taking over as "the teacher of record" just before the Winter Break was a daunting task, but I knew that building positive relationships with my students and their families was of utmost importance, especially considering I was joining the staff mid-year. I firmly believe that no matter how exceptional your curriculum or instructional skills may be, none of it matters if students don't feel that your classroom

is a safe space for them to learn and make mistakes.

By mistakes, I mean going through the process of learning, experiencing trials and errors, and taking risks by sharing their ideas. Students won't readily accept constructive criticism or coaching unless they know it comes from a place of care and support. That's why building positive relationships is key. It takes time, though. It took a few months after I arrived before I genuinely felt like I knew my students, their families, and the community around our school building. To establish those connections, I made sure to get involved in various ways. I volunteered for carpool duty, walked students home, accompanied them on an overnight camping trip, and made frequent positive phone calls to their homes. I seized every opportunity to speak with parents and build trust. It was an investment that paid off when it came to having difficult conversations later in the year. By then, students and parents knew that I genuinely cared about their well-being and that my classroom was a safe space for them to take intellectual risks. I firmly believe in the words of Ronald Ferguson, "We care; therefore they learn."

Furthermore, I strongly advocate incorporating real-world examples, culturally diverse materials, and project-based learning experiences into our teaching practices. Teachers should be familiar with "windows and mirrors (and sliding glass doors)" in instruction. It's about making learning relevant and connecting it to students' lives and experiences. Lessons should act as "windows" through which students learn about others and "mirrors" in which their own lives are reflected. Unfortunately, many curricula in K-12 classrooms have historically focused more on offering windows than mirrors. A lack of diverse perspectives has been represented, and that needs to change.

Sometimes, I hear math and science teachers dismiss the mirror component, saying things like "Math is math" or "Physics is physics." But even these subjects can be made relevant to students' lives. It can be as simple as incorporating their names, neighborhood landmarks, or favorite movie or TV characters into word problems. Finding real-world applications of math concepts is another effective way to make them relatable. The same goes for science. We need to go beyond the names mentioned in the textbooks and explore the diverse group of scientists and mathematicians who have made significant contributions throughout history.

Moreover, I firmly believe that the experts we need are already sitting in our classrooms. Many of our students have traveled the world and speak English as an additional language. Their lives are filled with valuable experiences and knowledge. As teachers, we need to take the time to get to know our students and incorporate their lives into our lessons. By doing so, we tap into their expertise and make learning more inclusive and relevant.

In conclusion, fostering connections with students and connecting learning to their lives is a superpower that teacher teams possess. By building positive relationships and making learning relevant, we create nurturing and inclusive classroom environments where students can thrive academically and personally. This year has reinforced the power of these approaches, and I am committed to continuing this journey of empowerment and growth with my students.[116]

Sarah Trevino—Fostering Connections and Unleashing Unlimited Potential: The High-Five Buddy Program's Impact on Student Success

Sarah Trevino is one of if not the best school counselors I have ever worked with. Her expertise in helping staff connect and build relationships with students is second to none. I asked Sarah to share in this

116. Taylor, Greg, personal communication (email), June 2023.

section about the "High Five Buddy" program she helped to develop at Mount Eagle Elementary when I was there as the principal. Here is what Sarah had to say:

> The High Five Buddy program at Mount Eagle ES was initiated in the fall of 2008 to provide additional positive adult relationships for our students. At that time, an existing mentoring program was already in place, matching staff members with students who would benefit from this extra support. However, while organizing the mentoring program for the year, we realized that all children would benefit from having an additional positive adult relationship, which led to the creation of the High Five Buddy program.
>
> Unlike the mentoring program, the High Five Buddy program was designed to be less time-consuming but impactful. Each staff member was paired with 6-7 students who would be their buddies throughout the year. The role of a staff buddy was to reveal themselves during an assigned week and, whenever they saw their student, give them a high five and a quick check-in to offer encouragement. The matching process was primarily random, but we considered classroom teachers to ensure proximity in classes or recess schedules. It's important to note that all staff members, including teachers, resource staff, office and building staff, and administrators, had high-five buddies. The program aimed to be inclusive, accessible, and low-stress while fostering a strong sense of community and building relationships.
>
> After the matches were made at the beginning of each school year, we had a designated week for staff members to introduce themselves to their buddies. There was no specific format for the introduction. Some staff members left notes on their buddy's desk, others would pull them out of class to say hello, and some would inform them in passing. As the years went

on, this week became something students looked forward to. They would come to my office excitedly, sharing if they knew who their buddy was or if they were still waiting to find out. I would also send a list to teachers, so they knew their students' assigned buddies in case anyone had trouble finding their way to the class. What struck me the most was the joy and impact of having a buddy who offered high fives and encouragement to our students; by incorporating inclusive practices into every student's day, even through simple gestures, we ensured that no one missed out on an opportunity that could have a lasting impact.

Having a High Five Buddy created a stronger sense of community for our students beyond the confines of the classroom. It made them feel seen and acknowledged beyond their academic performance. While this is typically the purpose of a mentoring program, we believed that all students deserved to have someone extra in their corner. The High Five Buddy program enabled us to include all students in fostering connections within the school. Additionally, it allowed staff members to build relationships with students they might not have interacted with regularly due to their specific roles. It was heartening to hear staff members discussing their check-ins with their buddies throughout the year or to see students stopping by the main office at the end of the day to give the administrative assistant a high five. These interactions demonstrated that the program successfully nurtured the connections we had hoped for.

The belief in every student's unlimited potential is crucial in education. When we view students in this light and provide them with the necessary support to access higher learning levels, their futures become limitless. Implementing practices and programs like the High Five Buddy program instills in students and staff that each matters and is valued for who they are and that everyone has something valuable to offer. Our unwavering belief in the unlimited potential of our students profoundly impacts all our outcomes, and the daily steps we take to convey this message to our students and staff are essential in creating a learning environment where every student can thrive.[117]

"As with the identification and activation of strengths...the catalytic power of relationships on intelligence is that the emotions emanating from relationships stimulate both the motivation and the memory capacity needed for learning."

—FEUERSTEIN ET AL.[118]

Many of you already use various strategies to build relationships with students. The goal is to establish a connection and create an emotional bond that encourages them to reciprocate. Remember when you successfully made a connection or built a relationship that positively impacted a student's life? As you engage with the "Thought Spark Questions," acknowledge and celebrate your journey, and reflect on how you can add more tools to your toolkit.

Thought Spark Questions: Fostering Connections and Connecting Learning: Empowering Students Through Relationships and Relevance

1. How do positive teacher-student relationships impact motivation and academic success?

2. What strategies foster strong connections and meaningful student relationships?

3. How can real-world examples and diverse materials enhance lesson relevance and inclusivity?

4. How do you encourage student reflection and expression?

5. How can active listening and empathy promote trust and

---

117. Trevino, Sarah, personal communication (email), July 2023.
118. Jackson, Yvette. *The Pedagogy of Confidence*. Teachers College Press, 2011, p. 93.

belonging?

6. What methods reinforce student achievements in the classroom?

7. How do collaboration and group projects boost engagement and teamwork?

Examples:

Pre-Year Home Visits: Teachers meet students and families at home for a personal connection.

Home-Based Parent-Teacher Conferences: Meetings at home strengthen parent-teacher partnerships.

Engaging Icebreaker Activities: Start with activities for student sharing.

Personalized Check-Ins: One-on-one conversations for tailored support.

Collaborative Endeavors: Projects encourage teamwork and idea exchange.

Student Reflection Platforms: Platforms for student expression and insights.

Affirmative Acknowledgment: Recognize student achievements for motivation.

Empathetic Active Listening: Build trust through genuine engagement and empathy.

Implementing these strategies can build strong student-teacher connections for academic and personal growth.

Elevating High Cognitive Performance

It all starts with expectations and beliefs. If we believe and expect that students will learn at high levels, and we put the tools in our toolkit to develop our superpowers, then students will learn at high levels. By implementing strategies such as Project-Based Learning (PBL), Socratic Seminars, and Open-Ended Assignments, teacher teams can challenge students to think critically and reach their full potential.

Here's a Story...
No Limits Middle School

At **No Limits Middle School**, a collaborative team of educators consisting of Maria Nielsen, Clara Sales, Aaron Hansen, and Regina Owens comes together to elevate high cognitive performance in English and social studies at the same grade level. With a shared commitment to student success, these teachers collaborate closely, sharing strategies and best practices and planning lessons together.

Maria Nielsen, an English and social studies teacher, brings her expertise in project-based learning to the team. She believes in engaging students through hands-on activities, research projects, and collaborative problem-solving tasks. By incorporating these strategies into their lessons, Maria encourages critical thinking and fosters a deep understanding of both subjects.

Clara Sales, also an English and social studies teacher, emphasizes the power of Socratic seminars to facilitate meaningful discussions among students. Clara's expertise is creating a safe and inclusive space where students can share their thoughts, challenge assumptions, and develop analytical skills. Through these seminars, students gain a deeper appreciation for literature and history while honing their communication abilities.

Aaron Hansen, an English and social studies teacher, brings his passion for open-ended assignments to the team. Aaron encourages creativity and independent thinking by allowing students to explore their interests and express their understanding in unique ways. His expertise in designing flexible assessments ensures that students can demonstrate their knowledge effectively.

Regina Owens, an English and social studies teacher, values the collaborative planning process with her team. Together, they discuss curriculum alignment, identify cross-curricular connections, and create integrated units of study. Through their collaboration, Regina ensures a cohesive learning experience for their students, promoting a deeper understanding of both English and social studies concepts.

Maria, Clara, Aaron, and Regina meet regularly as a team to share strategies and practices, exchange lesson ideas, and support one another. They collectively analyze student work, reflect on their teaching approaches, and adjust to meet their learners' evolving needs. Their collaborative efforts enable them to provide a well-rounded educational experience encompassing both English and social studies.

Through their dedication, these teachers create a dynamic learning environment where students thrive academically and personally. By integrating project-based learning, Socratic seminars, open-ended assignments, and collaborative planning, they foster a love for learning and critical thinking skills and a deep appreciation for the subjects they teach.

The collective efforts of Maria Nielsen, Clara Sales, Aaron Hansen, and Regina Owens showcase the power of collaboration and its impact on student achievement. Their commitment to elevating high cognitive performance in English and social studies creates a comprehensive learning experience that prepares students for future success.

Thought Spark Questions: Elevating High Cognitive Performance

1. How can setting high expectations and beliefs about student learning contribute to elevating high cognitive performance in English and social studies classrooms?

2. What are some effective strategies for implementing project-based learning, Socratic seminars, and open-ended assignments to challenge students to think critically?

3. How can collaborative planning and sharing of strategies among teachers, such as the team of Maria Nielsen, Clara Sales, Aaron Hansen, and Regina Owens, enhance student learning experiences in both English and social studies?

4. In what ways can Socratic seminars create a safe and inclusive space for students to share their thoughts, challenge assumptions, and develop analytical skills in English and social studies classes?

5. How does integrating project-based learning, open-ended assignments, and collaborative planning foster a love for learning, critical thinking skills, and a deeper appreciation for English and social studies subjects among students?

Offering Enhanced Learning Experiences

"Create space for genius, and genius will emerge."
—GHOLDY MUHAMMAD

The strategic approach of providing enhanced learning experiences empowers groups of teachers, including those in art, music, physical education, the library, and other non-core subjects, to collaboratively tailor education for their students' diverse needs and interests. These teachers and teams can develop strategies to enrich learning by identifying and leveraging student interests to engage students in activities that foster problem-solving, critical thinking, and challenging tasks. In essence, enhanced learning experiences encompass any activities that captivate students' attention and encourage them to actively challenge their minds. Importantly, teacher teams and other educators should collaborate creatively to design activities that align with students' interests, ensuring a well-rounded and engaging educational experience. This may involve implementing advanced coursework, coordinating intraschool curricular activities like clubs, and inviting inspirational role models to speak to the students.

Here's a Story...
Growth Mindset Elementary School

At Growth Mindset Elementary School, the fifth-grade team, consisting of Chris Jerry, Charles Brooks, Christy Yarn, and Nardos King, collaboratively organizes clubs during the school day to provide enrichment opportunities for all students. Recognizing the importance of offering diverse experiences, the team sets aside dedicated days each month for these clubs, with Chris taking the lead. They combine their expertise and contributions to create a well-rounded learning experience for their students.

A valued team member, Charles Brooks brings his expertise to advanced coursework. He ensures that advanced materials and assignments are accessible to all students, providing scaffolding and support as needed. Charles' commitment to differentiation and deep understanding of the subject matter enriches the overall learning experience for fifth-grade students.

Another key team member, Christy Yarn, contributes her expertise in organizing guest speaker sessions. She connects with professionals from various fields and arranges engaging sessions for the students. Christy's ability to bring real-world experiences into the classroom broadens students' perspectives and inspires their learning journey.

Nardos King, an integral part of the fifth-grade team, excels in designing interdisciplinary projects and activities. She incorporates critical thinking and creativity into their curriculum, ensuring students are challenged and engaged. Nardos' innovative approach and collaborative nature greatly enhance the learning experience for all fifth-grade students.

Through their collaboration and combined expertise, the fifth-grade team at Growth Mindset Elementary School creates an inclusive learning environment where every student can thrive. They provide equal opportunities for all students to access enrichment experiences, offering advanced coursework with scaffolding and support to those who may need it. By integrating clubs, guest speaker sessions, and interdisciplinary projects, the team provides a well-rounded education that nurtures the growth and success of all fifth-grade students.

In addition to their collaboration within the fifth-grade team, Chris Jerry, Charles Brooks, Christy Yarn, and Nardos King also work closely with other educators at Growth Mindset Elementary School to offer a comprehensive range of enriching experiences during the school day. They collaborate with the music, art, and physical education teachers as well as the strings teacher and band teacher to create a well-rounded educational experience for their students.

By collaborating with the music teacher, students can explore their musical talents and interests. They can participate in choir, learn to play an instrument, and engage in musical performances. This collaboration adds a creative and expressive element to their learning experience.

Working alongside the art teacher, students engage in various artistic endeavors. They learn different techniques, experiment with different mediums, and develop artistic skills. The collaboration with the art teacher allows students to express themselves creatively and appreciate the beauty of visual arts.

Collaborating with the physical education teacher ensures that students have regular physical activity and develop their physical skills. Students engage in various sports and activities, promoting physical fitness, teamwork, and sportsmanship. This collaboration emphasizes the importance of a well-rounded education that includes academic and physical development.

The strings and band teachers contribute to the enriching experiences by offering opportunities for students to learn to play musical instruments. Through collaboration, the fifth-grade team ensures that students interested in strings or band can pursue their musical interests and receive guidance and support in their musical journey.

By collaborating with other educators in the school, the fifth-grade team at Growth Mindset Elementary School provides their students with a holistic and well-rounded education. The combined efforts of the team and their fellow teachers ensure that students have access to a wide range of enriching experiences, fostering their growth, creativity, and physical well-being.

Thought Spark Questions: Offering Enhanced Learning Experiences

1. How can teacher teams at your school collaborate to provide enrichment opportunities catering to students' diverse needs and interests?

2. How can advanced coursework be made accessible to all students, including those who may need additional scaffolding and support?

3. How can guest speaker sessions be organized to bring real-world experiences into the classroom and broaden students' perspectives?

4. What strategies can be implemented to design interdisciplinary projects and activities that foster critical thinking and creativity among students?

5. How can collaboration with colleagues from other disciplines, such as music, art, physical education, strings, and band, enhance the overall learning experience for students and promote a well-rounded education?

6. What methods can ensure equal opportunities for all students to access enrichment experiences, regardless of their starting point or abilities?

7. Reflecting on the fifth-grade team's collaborative efforts, how might you integrate similar practices into your teaching to enhance students' learning experiences?

Identifying Prerequisites to Ensure Learning

Teacher teams possess the superpower to integrate prerequisites for learning seamlessly into their instruction. By collaborating and aligning their curriculum, teacher teams can ensure students have a strong foundation before progressing to more complex topics.

Here's a Story...
Collective Responsibility Career & Tech High

At Collective Responsibility Career & Tech High, the faculty members form a dynamic and passionate teacher team consisting of Mike Brown, Monica Butler, Kenny Barer, Paul Butler Jr., Mike O'Reilly, Darryl Webster, and Steve Frick. Together, they are dedicated to delivering an exceptional video production program that empowers their students for future success.

Understanding the significance of collective responsibility, this cohesive team leverages their combined knowledge, skills, wisdom, and expertise to benefit every student under their care. They believe in the importance of laying a solid foundation for learning before delving into more complex topics. To achieve this, they seamlessly integrate prerequisites into their instruction, ensuring that students have the necessary background knowledge before tackling advanced concepts.

One of the essential tools they use is pre-assessments. At the start of each course or unit, the teacher team collaboratively designs assessments to identify individual students' knowledge gaps and skill deficits. These pre-assessments provide valuable insights into where each student stands in their video production understanding.

Once they have identified these areas of need, the teacher team develops targeted interventions and support mechanisms to address them. No student is left behind, and every challenge is met with a tailored solution. In this spirit of inclusivity, the team welcomes special education teachers and English Language teachers as integral members. Their expertise ensures that students on their caseloads and those requiring extra support receive the necessary specialized instruction and accommodations.

The teacher team's dedication to collaboration extends beyond just pre-assessments and interventions. They work closely aligning their curricula to create a cohesive and inclusive learning experience for all. Their collective efforts result in a nurturing environment where students can flourish in video production.

Through their commitment to collaboration and inclusivity, this teacher team demonstrates the superpower of integrating prerequisites seamlessly. They create an environment where students learn the technical aspects of video production and develop essential skills, enabling them to overcome challenges and tap into their unique strengths, passions, and talents.

As the school year progresses, the impact of the teacher team's efforts becomes evident. Students' confidence grows, creativity blossoms, and their video production abilities reach new heights. The collective expertise of the teachers ensures that every student has the support they need to excel in their video production journey.

At Collective Responsibility Career & Tech High, the teacher team's unwavering dedication to their students' success continues to shape the future of aspiring video producers, preparing them to make a positive impact in the world through their storytelling and technical prowess.

Thought Spark Questions: Identifying Prerequisites to Ensure Learning

1. How can teacher teams collaborate effectively to identify and integrate prerequisites seamlessly into their instructional approach?

2. What strategies can educators use to design pre-assessments that effectively identify individual students' knowledge gaps, skill deficits, and areas that need extended because a student is already proficient in a specific subject area?

3. How can teacher teams ensure that targeted support, interventions, and extensions are tailored to meet the unique needs of each student, fostering inclusivity and promoting academic growth?

4. How can educators leverage the expertise of specialized teachers, such as special education and English Language teachers, to provide individualized instruction and accommodations for all students learning needs?

5. Reflecting on the story of the teacher team at Collective Responsibility Career & Tech High, how can educators create a cohesive and nurturing learning environment where students can thrive in video production and other subject areas?

ACKNOWLEDGING DIFFERENT POINTS OF ENTRY INTO THE CURRICULUM

Here's a Story...
Enter the Door Here Elementary School

TIERED TASKS
SUPPORTING EACH STUDENT'S ENTRY POINT INTO GRADE LEVEL CURRICULUM

In **Enter the Door Here Elementary School,** the third-grade teachers were passionate about providing their students with an enriching and personalized learning experience. The concept of tiered tasks had become the cornerstone of their teaching philosophy, as they believed in supporting each student's unique entry point into the grade-level curriculum.

In the heart of the school, Mrs. Thompson, Mrs. Ramirez, and Mr. Baldermann formed an extraordinary team of educators. They were dedicated to their profession and deeply committed to fostering a love for learning in their students. Their classrooms became havens of exploration, where every child was encouraged to tap into their unlimited potential.

The school year began with excitement and anticipation, and the teacher team eagerly collaborated to set their plans in motion. Understanding their students' diverse backgrounds and learning levels, they knew a one-size-fits-all approach wouldn't do. They had witnessed the power of tiered tasks in previous years and were eager to integrate it again into their curriculum.

One Monday morning, Mrs. Thompson gathered her students around a reading nook to introduce the concept of tiered tasks. "Today," she beamed, "we're diving into the fascinating world of multiplication. But remember, we all learn in different ways and at different paces. So, we'll explore multiplication together, but you'll be free to choose the level that suits you best!"

Her students' eyes sparkled with curiosity and excitement. With a sense of empowerment, they dove into the realm of multiplication. Some eagerly tackled one-by-one-digit problems, while others felt ready to venture into one-by-two-digit challenges. A few daring souls even opted for two-by-two-digit multiplication, eager to embrace the opportunity to challenge themselves.

In the classroom next door, Mrs. Ramirez was on a similar journey. Her students sat in a circle as she introduced tiered tasks with a big smile. "Today, my math wizards, we're going to unlock the secrets of multiplication. You all have the power to choose the level that feels right for you. And guess what? There's no such thing as too easy or too hard—it's all about finding your sweet spot!"

Excitement buzzed through the room as the students immersed themselves in the world of multiplication. Some confidently dived into two-by-two-digit problems, feeling assured in their skills. Others chose one-by-two-digit tasks, while a few started with one-by-one-digit multiplication to solidify their foundation. Mrs. Ramirez's heart swelled with pride as she witnessed her students enthusiastically embracing the challenge.

Meanwhile, Mr. Baldermann's class atmosphere was alive with curiosity. Mr. Baldermann, a firm believer in nurturing a growth mindset, began the day with an inspiring speech. "Today, young mathematicians, we embark on a journey through multiplication. Remember, you can choose the level that matches your readiness. Mistakes are learning opportunities, so let's embrace this adventure together!"

His students felt empowered as they tackled multiplication problems at their chosen level. Some opted for two-by-three-digit tasks, eager to push their boundaries and explore new horizons. Others decided to work on two-by-two-digit multiplication, while a few felt more comfortable refining their skills with one-by-two-digit problems.

Throughout the year, the teacher team collaborated and communicated regularly to ensure that their tiered approach was effectively supporting each student's growth. They celebrated every milestone, big or small, and provided additional support and resources to those who needed it.

By the end of the school year, the students had made remarkable progress, each on their unique path to mastery of essential grade-level curriculum and for many beyond. Tiered tasks had transformed their learning experience, empowering them to embrace challenges and discover their unlimited potential.

As the final bell rang on the last day of school, Mrs. Thompson, Mrs. Ramirez, and Mr. Baldermann gathered with pride. They knew that they had not only supported each student's entry point into the grade-level curriculum but also ignited a lifelong love for learning in their young students. Tiered tasks had been the catalyst for growth and transformation, ensuring that every student had the opportunity to flourish and unleash their unlimited potential.

Thought Spark Questions: Acknowledging Different Points of Entry into the Curriculum

1. How did the concept of tiered tasks in this story cater to each student's readiness? Provide examples from the narrative.

2. Reflect on the importance of allowing students to choose their own learning level within the expected grade level standard when tackling new subjects. How did this approach impact their motivation and confidence throughout the story?

3. In what ways did the teachers in the story foster a growth mindset among their students? How did this mindset contribute to the students' overall progress and success?

4. Describe the benefits of a collaborative teacher team that implements tiered tasks in the classroom. How did the teachers support each other and ensure access to grade level standards to each student?

5. Think about your own learning experiences. How might the use of tiered tasks be helpful in your current grade level and subject areas? How could this approach empower you to achieve your unlimited potential in your learning journey?

6. By considering thought spark questions, teacher teams can explore strategies to acknowledge and accommodate different points of entry into the grade level curriculum, ensuring that all students have equitable opportunities to succeed and thrive in their learning journeys.

CREATING A FLEXIBLE CLASSROOM

Here's a Story...
Stretch Middle School

Stretch Middle School, with its motto "Where Everyone Is Flexible," was where students embraced the superpower of creating flexible classrooms. The dedicated teacher team of five, known for their collective efficacy, came together to ensure that all students could thrive in a learning environment tailored to their needs.

Ms. Rodriguez, the math teacher, believed in creating a flexible classroom that supported individualized learning paths. She assessed her students' prior knowledge and readiness levels, then designed differentiated lessons and activities that catered to their unique needs. She ensured every student could progress by administering ongoing formative assessments and providing immediate feedback, building a solid foundation in mathematics.

Mr. Johnson, the English teacher, recognized the importance of accommodating different learning preferences in his classroom. He provided various modalities of instruction, allowing students to engage with the material through reading, listening, and kinesthetic activities. By incorporating multimedia resources, group discussions, and hands-on projects, Mr. Johnson fostered an inclusive environment where all students could connect with and comprehend the content.

Ms. Chen, the science teacher, understood the value of creating a flexible classroom that supported diverse learning needs. She implemented flexible grouping strategies to allow students to collaborate with peers at different readiness levels. Ms. Chen encouraged mutual support and learning by pairing students with complementary strengths based on assessment data. She also facilitated small-group activities and provided targeted interventions to address individual learning gaps, ensuring all students could participate actively and succeed in science.

Mr. Patel, the social studies teacher, embraced the idea of a flexible classroom that catered to different learning preferences. He implemented project-based learning experiences where students could choose topics of personal interest and demonstrate their understanding through various mediums, such as written reports, visual presentations, or even creative performances. Mr. Patel nurtured a sense of autonomy and ownership in their learning by providing multiple pathways for students to explore and express their knowledge.

Ms. Lewis, the physical education teacher, infused the super-power of creating a flexible classroom into her teaching practice by designing her lessons to accommodate different abilities, and interests. Through various sports and activities, she provided students with options based on their preferences and encour-aged them to set personal fitness goals. By fostering a supportive and non-competitive environment, Ms. Lewis ensured that all students could engage in physical activity and experience success, regardless of their individual strengths or challenges.

As the educators gathered to reflect on their practices, they further explored ways to enhance their flexible classroom envi-ronments. They discussed steps to create a learning space that supported individualized learning paths, catered to different learning preferences, and ensured every student could thrive. The reflection question "What steps can we take to create a flexible classroom environment that supports individualized learning paths and caters to different learning preferences?" guided their discussion, inspiring them to continue unleashing their collective teaching superpowers for the benefit of all their students.

At Stretch Middle School, the teacher team embraced the superpower of creating flexible classrooms, empowering stu-dents to learn in a way that best suits their needs. Their collective efficacy and commitment to personalized instruction created an inclusive and nurturing environment where everyone could thrive and tap into their unlimited potential. The motto "Where Everyone is Flexible" came to life as students embraced their unique learning journeys, supported by a team of educators dedicated to their success.

Examples:

1. Offering flexible seating options, such as standing desks, bean bags, or floor cushions, to accommodate different

learning preferences and allow students to choose a seating arrangement that suits their needs.

2. Implementing a variety of instructional modalities, such as videos, hands-on activities, group discussions, and online resources, to cater to diverse learning styles and engage students with different preferences for how they absorb and process information.

3. Utilizing flexible grouping strategies, such as collaborative learning groups or ability-based groupings, provides opportunities for students to work with peers at different readiness levels and support one another's learning.

4. Providing choice in assignments and assessments, allowing students to select topics or projects that align with their interests and strengths, fostering a sense of ownership and motivation in their learning.

5. Incorporating technology tools and resources that offer flexibility in accessing content, allowing students to work at their own pace, revisit material as needed, and explore additional resources to deepen their understanding.

Thought Spark Questions: Creating a Flexible Classroom

1. How can we establish clear expectations and provide choices to create a flexible classroom environment that empowers students to take ownership of their learning?

2. What strategies can we implement to incorporate varied grouping strategies and personalized learning paths that cater to the diverse needs of our learners?

3. How can we utilize flexible seating options to create a positive classroom climate and accommodate different learning preferences and styles?

4. What resources and materials can we provide to support individualized learning paths and ensure that all students can access the necessary tools for success?

5. How can we collaborate as a teacher team to share effective practices, refine our instructional approaches, and continuously improve our ability to create a flexible classroom that meets the needs of every student?

By harnessing their extraordinary superpowers, teacher teams transform the learning landscape. They appreciate student strengths, forge connections, promote high-level thinking, provide engaging experiences, address individual needs, accommodate diverse entry points, and foster flexibility. With these powers, teacher teams cultivate an inclusive and empowering educational environment that allows students to flourish.

Just as teacher teams possess many superpowers, students, too, have unlimited potential waiting to be unlocked. By harnessing their strengths and perspectives, students can actively participate in shaping their learning experiences. Empowering students to recognize and utilize their strengths allows them to become active participants in their education, fostering a sense of ownership and pride in their achievements.

The Students' Superpowers

FOSTERING CONFIDENCE IN STUDENTS WITH 7 ESSENTIAL ATTRIBUTES

Numerous esteemed authors have delved into the realm of attributes crucial for students to develop to become adaptable and adept individuals. In their respective work, these authors highlight vital qualities necessary for thriving in today's multifaceted world. For instance, *Growing Tomorrow's Citizens in Today's Classrooms* (2019) by Cassandra Erkens, Tom

Schimmer, and Nicole Dimich identifies "7 Critical Competencies."[119] Art Costa's *Learning and Leading with Habits of Mind* (2008) outlines sixteen distinctive characteristics.[120] Michelle Borba's *Thrivers* (2022) discusses "7 Essential Traits.[121] And Daniel Goleman's groundbreaking *Emotional Intelligence: Why It Can Matter More Than IQ* (1995) addresses indispensable skills.[122]

Although these authors present varying terminologies, their core significance remains aligned. For instance, Daniel Goleman refers to "self-management," while Michelle Borba employs "self-control." In this context, these terms can be considered synonymous.

Furthermore, these attributes are typically cultivated over time, rather than being innate or automatic. They are honed through experience, training, and conscious effort, exerting profound influence on personal outcomes and interactions. These attributes mold an individual's approach to others, their handling of situations, and the pursuit of goals.

It is crucial to recognize that these attributes are not rigid traits; they can be cultivated, refined, and transformed through deliberate practice, introspection, and personal growth initiatives. Educators play a pivotal role by delivering explicit instruction and setting positive examples.

While the list of attributes presented here is not exhaustive, it is informed by my years of work and experience. These attributes provide students with essential tools to cultivate confidence when dealing with and overcoming challenging situations in their educational journey and in life.

This section delves into seven essential attributes that hold significant importance in nurturing students from Pre-K through the twelfth grade.

119. Erkens, Cassandra, et al., *Growing Tomorrow's Citizens in Today's Classrooms: Assessing Seven Critical Competencies*, Solution Tree Press, 2019.

120. Costa, Arthur, *Learning and Leading with Habits of Mind: 16 Essential Characteristics for Success*, ASCD, 2008.

121. Borba, Michelle, *Thrivers: The Surprising Reasons Why Some Kids Struggle and Others Shine*, Putnam and Sons, 2021.

122. Goleman, Daniel, *Emotional Intelligence: Why It Can Matter More Than IQ*. Bantam Books, 1995.

Each attribute represents a unique aspect of a well-rounded individual, empowering learners to overcome hurdles, embrace change, and confidently approach uncertainties. As these attributes become ingrained, they transform into powerful assets for students, arming them with the ability to tackle challenges with certainty and the expectation of successful outcomes.

1. Persisting
2. Precise Thinking and Communication
3. Self-control
4. Empathy
5. Curiosity
6. Thinking Flexibly
7. Optimism and Hope

First, we explore the superpower of **persisting**. Through cultivating a growth mindset, we help students understand that setbacks are not roadblocks but stepping stones toward success.

Next, we delve into **precise thinking and communication**, recognizing the value of clear and compelling expression in all facets of life.

We then focus on **self-control**, highlighting its pivotal role in emotional regulation and impulse management. By cultivating self-awareness and self-discipline, students can make informed choices, control their reactions, and maintain their composure in challenging situations.

Empathy, highlighted in this section, enables students to understand and share the feelings of others. By fostering empathy, we equip students with the capacity to build meaningful relationships, resolve conflicts, and contribute positively to their communities, fostering a sense of social responsibility.

Curiosity promotes a thirst for knowledge, a passion for exploration, and the desire to understand the world around them. Encouraging students to question and explore empowers them to become active learners, critical thinkers, and problem solvers in an ever-changing world.

Thinking flexibly, the second to last attribute, equips students with the cognitive agility to adapt their thinking and approaches when faced with new challenges. By embracing diverse perspectives and exploring alternative solutions, students develop a mental resilience that allows them to navigate uncertainties and complexities easily.

This section concludes with **Optimism** (hope), highlighting its transformative power in shaping students' outlook on life. By fostering a positive mindset, we empower students to see opportunities in every setback, to maintain hope in the face of adversity, and to approach challenges with unwavering determination.

This section provides brief fictional stories based on my professional experiences that can be integrated into educational settings at any level to cultivate these essential attributes. Teachers will need to adjust depending on the developmental stage of the students and the content that is being taught. By empowering Pre-K-12 students with these foundational skills, we aim to equip them with the resilience, adaptability, and the mindset necessary to face obstacles successfully, paving the way for success in school and lifelong success and fulfillment.

PERSISTING

"Nothing in this world can take the place of persistence. Talent will not; nothing is more common than unsuccessful men with talent. Genius will not; unrewarded genius is almost a proverb. Education will not; the world is full of educated derelicts. Persistence and determination alone are omnipotent. The slogan 'Press On!' has solved and always will solve the problems of the human race."

—CALVIN COOLIDGE[123]

---

123. "Calvin Coolidge," Goodreads, https://www.goodreads.com/quotes/2749-nothing-in-this-world-can-take-the-place-of-persistence.

Chapter 1 revealed the close connection between dopamine, a neurotransmitter associated with motivation and pleasure, and persistence within the brain's reward system. Leveraging this knowledge, teacher teams can structure tasks and provide feedback that fosters a sense of accomplishment and reinforces students' persistence by actively engaging their dopamine release.

Here's a Story...
We Believe in You Middle School

At We Believe in You Middle School, an extraordinary teacher team of Saundra Green, Haywood Corley, Margaret McCourt-Dirner, Mike Cohen, and Meg Tuccillo recognized the transformative power of persisting and was determined to empower their students. One of their students, Rosa, often struggled with self-doubt and gave up too quickly.

The team understood the importance of cultivating the behavior and attitude of persisting in Rosa's journey. They created a nurturing and inclusive classroom environment led by Saundra as the team leader. Haywood and Margaret tailored their instructional approach to meet Rosa's specific needs, providing both challenge and support.

Mike, known for his enthusiasm, shared inspiring stories of individuals who achieved success through perseverance, instilling a belief in Rosa's own abilities. With her compassionate nature, Meg listened attentively and offered guidance whenever Rosa faced obstacles.

Implementing strategies to reinforce Rosa's persistence, the team introduced goal-setting exercises. They helped Rosa break tasks into manageable steps, celebrating each achievement. Saundra awarded "Persisting Stars" and Meg left heartfelt notes of encouragement on Rosa's desk, creating a culture of support.

The teacher team extended their efforts beyond the classroom, fostering a sense of community among students. They facilitated collaborative projects, pairing Rosa with classmates who excelled in areas where she struggled. This collaborative approach strengthened Rosa's persistence and cultivated meaningful friendships.

Over time, Rosa internalized the value of persisting. She witnessed her growth and realized that setbacks were stepping stones toward success. With the unwavering support of Saundra, Haywood, Margaret, Mike, and Meg, Rosa developed confidence and embraced challenges with resilience.

The transformation of Rosa became an inspiration within the "We Believe in You" Middle School community. The teacher team's commitment to empowering their students with the essential behavior and attitude of persisting profoundly impacted Rosa's life. With their guidance, she tapped into her unlimited potential, embracing a future filled with endless possibilities.

Persisting Examples:

- Implement long-term projects or challenges that require sustained effort, such as creating a class garden or organizing a charity event.

- Provide incremental rewards and celebrate milestones to maintain students' motivation and persistence.

- Assign complex tasks that require students to break them down into smaller steps, providing them with a sense of progress and achievement.

- Teach students strategies for managing frustration and setbacks, such as positive self-talk or seeking help when needed.

- Engage students in real-world problem-solving projects that require perseverance, such as designing a sustainable energy solution or organizing a community awareness campaign.
- Encourage students to reflect on their progress and growth throughout the project, reinforcing their persistence.

Thought Spark Questions: Persisting

1. How can we shift students' perspectives to view setbacks as opportunities for growth and learning, fostering a mindset of persistence?

2. What specific strategies can we employ to help students develop resilience and perseverance when faced with challenges?

3. How can we provide adequate support and guidance to students encountering difficulties, encouraging them to persist and overcome obstacles?

4. How can goal-setting and celebrating progress contribute to students' development of persistence and a belief in their capabilities?

5. What collaborative opportunities can we create for students to support each other in persisting through challenges, fostering a sense of community and mutual encouragement?

PRECISE THINKING AND COMMUNICATION

Here's a Story...
Clarity Precedes Competence Elementary School
MASCOT: "THE CLEAR THINKERS"

At Clarity Precedes Competence Elementary School, the preschool team consisting of Dr. Carolyn Miller, Lillie Jessie, Sylvia Taub, and Gloria Hoffman recognized the importance of supporting all preschool students, including those learning English as an additional language, in developing precise thinking and communication skills. They understood that visual cues were vital in facilitating understanding and enhancing communication for young learners.

Throughout their teaching practices, the team heavily relied on visuals to model concepts and instructions for all students. They created and utilized various visual aids such as charts, diagrams, illustrations, and flashcards. These visuals were powerful tools to accompany lessons and discussions, providing a clear and visual representation of the content.

During storytelling activities, the team incorporated visuals to complement the narratives. They used picture books, storyboards, and visual prompts to help students follow the plot, understand the sequence of events, and connect the meanings of words to visual representations. This approach fostered preschool students' comprehension, language development, and engagement.

When teaching vocabulary, the team employed visual flashcards and posters. They associated images with specific words, enabling students to establish connections between the visual representation and the corresponding term. Visual cues became instrumental in expanding students' vocabulary and reinforcing their understanding of new words, benefiting all learners in the classroom.

Moreover, the team integrated visual aids during various activities and projects. They encouraged students to create their own visuals, such as drawings, collages, and other visual mediums, to represent their ideas and demonstrate their understanding. Students were empowered to communicate their thoughts effectively and showcase their learning to their peers and teachers by incorporating visual artifacts.

The team's use of visual cues went beyond supporting English language learners. They recognized that visual aids benefited all preschool students, providing additional scaffolding and reinforcement for concepts, vocabulary, and communication skills. By incorporating visuals, Dr. Carolyn Miller, Lillie Jessie, Sylvia Taub, and Gloria Hoffman created an inclusive and supportive learning environment, where all students could develop precise thinking and effective communication abilities.

In learning about the brain in Chapter 1, the idea of clear and precise thinking is supported by different brain regions responsible for language processing, memory, and executive functions. Teacher teams can foster this skill by incorporating activities that enhance vocabulary, promote effective communication, and encourage students to articulate their thoughts.

Examples:

- Engage students in storytelling activities that require them to use descriptive language and express their ideas clearly.

- Provide opportunities for small group discussions where students can practice active listening and responding with clarity and precision.

- Teach students specific vocabulary related to different subjects and encourage them to use precise language in their written and oral presentations.

- Incorporate debates or structured discussions that require students to present well-reasoned arguments and respond to counterarguments.

- Assign research papers or projects that challenge students to communicate complex ideas clearly and concisely.

- Provide explicit instruction on effective presentation skills, including body language, tone of voice, and visual aids.

Thought Spark Questions: Precise Thinking & Communication

1. How can we emphasize the importance of clear and effective expression in various aspects of our students' lives, from preschool to grade twelve?

2. What instructional strategies can we employ to enhance students' critical thinking and communication skills across different grade levels and subjects?

3. How can we create diverse and engaging opportunities for students to practice and refine their communication abilities, considering students' developmental stages and learning needs from preschool to grade twelve?

4. In what ways can we effectively incorporate visual cues and aids to support precise thinking and communication skills in our classrooms, regardless of the grade level?

5. How can we foster a collaborative and inclusive learning environment that encourages active listening, responding with clarity and precision, and respectful communication among students of all ages?

6. What approaches can we take to provide explicit instruction on effective presentation skills, including body language, tone of voice, and visual aids, to enhance students' communication abilities throughout their educational journey?

7. How can we design and implement innovative projects or activities that challenge students across different grade levels to communicate complex ideas clearly and concisely, nurturing their precise thinking and communication skills?

SELF-CONTROL

*"Research shows that willpower is more important than IQ.
That's why the point isn't to become smarter but to become more
self-disciplined."*

—ADAM KIRK SMITH[124]

Self-control is a vital skill that empowers individuals to excel in various aspects of life. As we learned in Chapter 1, the prefrontal cortex, responsible for impulse control and executive functions, undergoes substantial development during adolescence. Teacher teams can play a crucial role in nurturing this development by offering explicit instruction on self-regulation techniques.

Here's a Story...
Prefrontal Cortex Independent School District

In the Prefrontal Cortex Independent School District (ISD), visionary leaders Edward Ayers, Betsy Fenske, William Ayers, and Chuck Ayers dedicated themselves to supporting schools and administrator teams in implementing strategies to develop the essential skill of self-control. Their collective efforts aimed to nurture self-regulation skills in students across the district, leveraging the power of the prefrontal cortex for improved academic achievement and overall well-being.

With his deep understanding of effective instructional practices, Edward Ayers collaborated closely with administrator teams to provide professional learning opportunities focused on teaching self-control. Through workshops and training sessions,

---

124. "Adam Kirk Smith," Goodreads, https://www.goodreads.com/author/quotes/15976168.Adam_Kirk_Smith.

administrators gained valuable insights and resources to guide teachers in implementing classroom self-control strategies.

Betsy Fenske, a passionate advocate for social-emotional learning, worked alongside administrator teams to create a nurturing and supportive school environment. They collaborated on developing positive behavior support plans, integrating moments of reflection and problem-solving activities, and establishing consistent expectations that fostered self-control and emotional regulation.

William Ayers, a proponent of student engagement, partnered with administrator teams to design engaging project-based learning experiences that promoted self-control. Together, they created long-term research projects and goal-setting initiatives that challenged students to exercise self-control while pursuing their academic goals.

Chuck Ayers, dedicated to building a positive school culture, worked hand in hand with administrator teams to implement schoolwide initiatives that celebrated and reinforced self-control. They established systems that recognized and rewarded students' self-regulation efforts, creating an environment where all valued and practiced self-control.

The collaborative efforts of Edward Ayers, Betsy Fenske, William Ayers, Charles Ayers, and the dedicated administrator teams in the Prefrontal Cortex ISD cultivated a culture of self-control. Schools became centers of self-regulation development, empowering students with the skills to manage their impulses, make thoughtful decisions, and thrive academically and personally.

Examples:

- Teach students calming techniques, such as deep breathing or counting to ten, to help them manage impulsive behaviors.

- Implement consistent classroom routines and visual schedules to provide students with a sense of structure and predictability.

- Incorporate mindfulness exercises or brief moments of reflection at the beginning or end of each class to help students regulate their emotions and impulses.

- Teach students problem-solving strategies that involve considering multiple solutions before acting impulsively.

- Provide opportunities for students to engage in activities that require delayed gratification, such as long-term research projects or goal setting.

- Foster a classroom culture that values thoughtful reflection and decision-making, encouraging students to think before acting.

Tracking, Assessing, Analyzing, and Responding

Self-control is a crucial skill for students to develop, and collecting data can help educators assess its progress and effectiveness. The teacher teams and administrators at Prefrontal Cortex ISD understood the importance of data-driven decision-making and utilized various methods to collect information on self-control.

Examples of data collection strategies include:

1. Observational Assessments: Teachers and administrators conducted regular classroom observations to gauge students' self-control behaviors in different situations. They used observation checklists or rubrics to track indicators such as impulse control, emotional regulation, and following directions.

2. Self-Reflection and Goal Setting: Students were encouraged to engage in self-reflection exercises and set personal goals related to self-control. Educators used journals or goal-setting sheets where students could document their progress and challenges, providing valuable insights into their self-regulation journey.

3. Behavior Tracking: Teachers implemented behavior tracking systems to monitor students' self-control in specific contexts or activities. They used tools like student goal cards or point systems to record instances of self-control and provide feedback to students.

4. Surveys and Questionnaires: Educators administered surveys or questionnaires to assess students' self-perception of their self-control skills. These self-report measures helped identify areas of strength and areas for improvement from the students' perspectives.

5. Academic Performance and Task Completion: The team also considered academic performance and task completion rates as indicators of self-control. They examined whether students could manage distractions, stay focused, and complete tasks promptly.

By analyzing and interpreting the data collected through these strategies, teacher teams and administrators gain valuable insights into the progress and challenges related to self-control. This data informed instructional adjustments, individualized support, and targeted interventions to further enhance students' self-control skills and foster a positive learning environment.

Thought Spark Questions: Self-Control

1. How can we effectively collaborate as a team to support the development of self-control skills in our students?

2. What steps can we take to align our instructional practices and strategies to promote a consistent approach to self-control across grade levels and subject areas?

3. What professional learning opportunities or resources can we provide to enhance our understanding and implementation of self-control strategies?

4. What data or evidence can we collect to assess the impact of our self-control initiatives and make informed adjustments to our strategies?

EMPATHY

"I think we all have empathy.
We may not have enough courage to display it."
—MAYA ANGELOU[125]

Here's a Story...
Empathy High School—The Caring Cubs

In the halls of Empathy High School—The Caring Cubs, teachers and administrators recognized empathy's incredible power. They sought to make it a cornerstone of their students' educations. Led by a passionate team of educators, including Mike Dunn, Cassie Guy, Ben Dashiell, and Nicole Walker, with the guidance of Michelle Moaney on the guiding coalition, the school was committed to nurturing the superpower of empathy in their students.

The teachers and administrators designed various activities and lessons throughout the school year to cultivate student empathy. They understood the importance of perspective-taking and provided opportunities for students to engage in role-playing, cooperative learning, and meaningful discussions that explored diverse viewpoints.

In small group activities, students were encouraged to share their personal experiences and perspectives while their peers

---

125. "May Angelou Quotes," BrainyQuote, https://www.brainyquote.com/quotes/maya_angelou_578832.

practiced active listening and empathy. These discussions created a safe space for students to express themselves and develop a deeper understanding of one another.

The school library was filled with books that highlighted characters from different backgrounds and cultures, allowing students to step into the shoes of others and gain a broader perspective. Teachers facilitated discussions around these stories, guiding students to connect with the characters' emotions and experiences.

Collaborative problem-solving tasks were assigned in classrooms, challenging students to consider multiple perspectives and find common ground. Structured debates and discussions on controversial topics were also held, promoting respectful listening and responding. These activities taught students how to engage in dialogue while understanding and appreciating different points of view.

Empathy extended beyond the school's walls through community service and volunteer projects. Students actively participated in initiatives that exposed them to various social issues, fostering compassion and a sense of social responsibility.

The school organized cross-cultural exchanges and dialogues to expand students' horizons further. These experiences allowed students to interact with individuals from different backgrounds, fostering empathy and understanding on a global scale.

The teachers and administrators at Empathy High School— The Caring Cubs continually reflected on their practices, seeking ways to deepen their students' empathy skills. They asked themselves thought-provoking questions such as how to foster empathy in students, what activities could promote empathy and social responsibility, and how to apply empathy in resolving conflicts and building positive relationships.

Through their dedication to nurturing empathy, Empathy High School—The Caring Cubs created a compassionate and inclusive learning environment, empowering students to connect with others on a deeper level and positively impact the world.

Empathy and perspective-taking enable individuals to understand and share others' emotions and experiences. Teacher teams can promote this skill by incorporating activities that encourage perspective-taking, such as role-playing, cooperative learning, and discussions exploring diverse viewpoints.

Other Examples for Consideration:

- Organize small group activities where students share their experiences and perspectives while others practice active listening and empathy.

- Read and discuss stories highlighting characters from different backgrounds and cultures, promoting empathy and understanding.

- Engage students in collaborative problem-solving tasks that require them to consider multiple perspectives and find common ground.

- Facilitate structured debates or discussions on controversial topics, encouraging respectful listening and responding.

- Incorporate community service or volunteer projects that expose students to different social issues and encourage empathy toward others.

- Provide opportunities for students to engage in cross-cultural exchanges or dialogues to broaden their perspectives and understanding.

Thought Spark Questions: Empathy

1. How can we create a safe and inclusive classroom environment that promotes empathy and understanding among our students?

2. What strategies can we incorporate into our lessons to encourage perspective-taking and help students develop empathy?

3. How can we integrate diverse perspectives and experiences into our curriculum to broaden students' understanding of others?

4. How can we foster empathy in students when resolving conflicts or building positive relationships?

5. How can we extend opportunities for community service and cross-cultural exchanges to deepen students' empathy and social responsibility?

CURIOSITY

"All kids are curious about everything. They overturn rocks and, you know, poke things, and generally create chaos at home. Most of what parents do is they spend the first years of the kids' life teaching them to walk and talk, and then the rest of life tell them to shut up and sit down.... If you retain that curiosity, that rampant curiosity, you're a scientist. A scientist is a kid who grew up physically but not emotionally, not mentally. And all scientists are like that."

—Neil deGrasse Tyson[126]

126. aiuniverseexplorer, Instagram (video), https://www.instagram.com/reel/CtkT-jWeA_K4/?igshid=ZTJlZmI4ZjZmNw%3D%3D.

Here's a Story...
Curious Owl Middle School

NICKNAMED "THE HOOTS"

Linda Layton, Reina Castillo, Laurentia Blay, and LaShawn Argabright, the passionate teacher team of Curious Owl Middle School, known as "The Hoots," gathered in the vibrant gymnasium, ready to unleash the superpower of curiosity in their students.

Inspired by Neil deGrasse Tyson's quote, they knew nurturing curiosity was key to engaging their students in physical activity and fostering a lifelong love for fitness and well-being. They wanted to create an environment where Curious Owl Middle School students could explore, discover, and question the world of physical education.

Linda, Reina, and Laurentia, the dedicated physical education teachers of The Hoots, brainstormed ways to integrate curiosity into their curriculum. At the same time, LaShawn, the big-picture person, ensured their ideas aligned with the overall vision of the school.

Linda, a fitness expert, proposed incorporating interactive games and challenges to ignite students' curiosity and encourage them to think creatively. "Let's design obstacle courses that require students to use their problem-solving skills and develop innovative ways to overcome obstacles," she suggested. "By embracing curiosity, they'll enjoy exploring new movements and strategies."

Reina, a skilled physical education teacher, added, "We can introduce sports and games from different cultures and periods to spark students' curiosity about the history and diversity of physical activities. By understanding the origins and traditions behind these sports, they'll develop a deeper appreciation and interest in physical education."

Laurentia, a health and wellness expert, said, "Let's incorporate discussions and projects that encourage students to explore the science behind exercise, nutrition, and the human body. We can nurture their curiosity about how physical activity impacts their well-being by posing thought-provoking questions and guiding their research."

LaShawn, the big-picture person, listened attentively and ensured the team's ideas aligned with the broader goals of Curious Owl Middle School and The Hoots. "Let's also create opportunities for students to set personal fitness goals and track their progress," LaShawn suggested. "By empowering them to take ownership of their physical health, we foster their curiosity to explore their unlimited potential and strive for continuous improvement."

The team's energy was contagious as they envisioned a physical education program that empowered Curious Owl Middle School students to be curious, active learners. They discussed integrating technology, such as fitness trackers and interactive apps, to engage students and provide opportunities for self-discovery.

They decided to incorporate regular reflection sessions to create a culture that valued and encouraged questioning, exploration, and problem-solving. These moments would allow students to share their experiences, ask questions, and explore new ideas related to physical education and personal fitness.

The team was filled with excitement and determination as they concluded their meeting. They were ready to inspire their students at Curious Owl Middle School to embrace physical education with wonder and curiosity. They knew that by nurturing the superpower of curiosity, they were promoting physical fitness and instilling a lifelong love for active, healthy living.

Together, Linda, Reina, Laurentia, and LaShawn, the dedicated teacher team of The Hoots, were on a mission to illuminate the force of curiosity within each student, unlocking their unlimited potential to become fit, resilient, and curious individuals who approached physical education with enthusiasm and a thirst for knowledge.

Examples:

- Integrate creative writing activities encouraging students to imagine and develop their own stories, characters, and settings.
- Incorporate art projects that allow students to explore different mediums, experiment with materials, and express their unique ideas.
- Assign open-ended research projects that require students to think creatively and develop innovative solutions to real-world problems.
- Encourage students to create and present original inventions or designs that address a specific need or challenge.
- Implement project-based learning experiences that allow students to tackle complex, authentic problems, encouraging creativity and innovation.
- Introduce entrepreneurship activities that challenge students to develop and pitch their business ideas, fostering creativity and critical thinking.

Thought Spark Questions: Curiosity

1. How can we inspire and nurture students' curiosity and passion for learning in our classrooms?
2. What strategies can we employ to foster curiosity, creativity, and imagination within our lessons and activities?

3. How can we create a culture that values and encourages questioning, exploration, and problem-solving among our students?

4. What activities or projects can we implement to stimulate divergent thinking and innovation in our curriculum?

5. How can we integrate elements of creativity, such as art, writing, or design, into our lessons to spark curiosity and foster self-expression?

6. What opportunities can we provide students to explore connections between different subjects or real-world applications, promoting curiosity and more profound understanding?

THINKING FLEXIBLY

"The measure of intelligence is the ability to change."

—ALBERT EINSTEIN[127]

Here's a Story...
Flexible Thinkers High School:

WE BEND BUT NEVER BREAK

The Guiding Coalition at Flexible Thinkers High School, consisting of Robert Ayers, Christine Sutton, Barbara Ayers, Jean Moaney, and Brenda Brittingham, empowered all staff members to support students in developing the superpower of Thinking Flexibly. Their collective efforts aimed to cultivate a schoolwide culture that fostered cognitive flexibility and adaptive thinking.

---

127. "Flexibility Quotes," Goodreads, https://www.goodreads.com/quotes/tag/flexibility.

Understanding the significance of flexible thinking in every facet of life, the Guiding Coalition recognized the need for all educators to be equipped with strategies and resources to nurture this skill in their students. They believed that by reframing traditional approaches to education, they could create an environment that embraced diverse perspectives, challenged preconceptions, and promoted cognitive flexibility.

As the principal and leader of the Guiding Coalition, Robert Ayers emphasized the importance of providing professional learning opportunities for staff members. He encouraged them to explore research and best practices for flexible thinking, adaptability, and neuroplasticity. Through workshops, collaborative discussions, and ongoing support, the coalition aimed to empower educators with the knowledge and skills to guide students in developing flexible thinking abilities.

Barbara Ayers, an influential team member and an experienced educator, worked closely with her colleagues to design instructional strategies that promoted flexible thinking. She encouraged teachers to incorporate open-ended questions, problem-solving activities, and real-world scenarios into their lessons. Engaging students in critical thinking, reflection, and exploring multiple perspectives fostered cognitive flexibility and encouraged them to adapt their thinking when faced with new challenges.

Jean Moaney, an advocate for interdisciplinary learning, collaborated with her fellow team members to integrate flexible thinking across subject areas. Designing cross-curricular projects and activities allowed students to apply flexible thinking skills in various contexts. This holistic approach reinforced the idea that flexible thinking is a transferable skill that transcends individual disciplines.

Christine Sutton, an innovative math teacher, focused on creating a classroom environment that encouraged experimentation, risk-taking, and the exploration of different problem-solving strategies. Through collaborative group work, students learned to appreciate diverse approaches and expand their thinking beyond traditional methods. Christine also promoted the use of technology tools and resources that facilitated flexible thinking and adaptive learning.

Brenda Brittingham, a passionate social studies teacher, worked alongside her coalition colleagues to infuse flexible thinking into the social studies curriculum. She incorporated simulations, role-playing activities, and case studies that challenged students to think critically, consider multiple perspectives, and adapt their thinking based on new information. Brenda also advocated for community partnerships and real-world experiences that exposed students to diverse viewpoints and fostered a greater understanding of global issues.

As the Guiding Coalition met to reflect on their collective efforts, they recognized the progress made in promoting flexible thinking throughout the school. They discussed how they could further enhance professional development opportunities, refine instructional strategies, and create a supportive network where all staff members felt empowered to embrace flexible thinking as an essential component of their teaching practice.

Together, the Guiding Coalition at Flexible Thinkers High School led the charge in transforming the school culture to one that valued and nurtured flexible thinking. Their collaborative efforts ensured that all educators had the tools, resources, and support necessary to empower students in developing this crucial superpower. By reframing traditional approaches and fostering a growth mindset, the guiding coalition and the entire school community were committed to equipping students with the skills to adapt, innovate, and thrive in an ever-changing world.

Neuroplasticity, the brain's ability to reorganize and form new neural connections, supports flexible thinking. Teacher teams can encourage flexible thinking by exposing students to diverse perspectives, challenging their preconceptions, and promoting cognitive flexibility through activities that require problem-solving and adapting to new situations.

Examples:

- Provide opportunities for students to explore different problem-solving strategies and encourage them to try alternative approaches.

- Introduce literature or stories that depict characters who demonstrate flexible thinking and adaptability.

- Engage students in activities that require them to solve puzzles, riddles, or brainteasers that encourage flexible thinking.

- Assign group projects that involve collaborative decision-making and require students to consider multiple perspectives and ideas.

- Incorporate real-world scenarios or case studies that involve complex problems, challenging students to think critically, evaluate options, and adjust their thinking accordingly.

- Offer opportunities for students to engage in simulations or role-playing exercises where they must navigate and continually assess and rethink their path.

Thought Spark Questions: Thinking Flexibly

1. How can we create a classroom environment that encourages students to adapt their thinking and approaches when faced with new challenges?

2. What instructional techniques or activities can we incorporate to promote flexible thinking and embrace diverse perspectives among our students?

3. In what ways can we foster a mindset of exploring alternative solutions and approaches to problem-solving within our classrooms?

OPTIMISM & HOPE

"Hope is often misunderstood. People tend to think that it is simply passive wishful thinking: I hope something will happen but I'm not going to do anything about it. This is indeed the opposite of real hope, which requires action and engagement."

—Jane Goodall[128]

Here's a Story...
Si Se Puede Pre-K-12 School District—
THE PLACE WHERE OPTIMISM AND HOPE REIGN

In the Si Se Puede Pre-K-12 school district, collaboration was not just a once-a-month occurrence during the Optimism Power Hour but a fundamental way of doing business. The educators understood that to foster optimism and hope in their students, they needed to continuously share strategies, ideas, and experiences with one another.

During grade-level team meetings and full staff learning sessions, and even informally throughout the day, the educators actively discussed their practices and approaches. They were encouraged and expected to share their successful strategies for cultivating a positive mindset in their classrooms. The exchange of ideas and experiences became a regular part of their professional learning and collective growth.

128. "63 Best Jane Goodall Quotes on Hope & Making a Difference," Goodreads, https://www.goodgoodgood.co/articles/jane-goodall-quotes.

In grade-level team meetings, the educators came together to discuss challenges they encountered and brainstorm solutions. They openly shared the strategies that had worked well for them and sought input from their colleagues. By leveraging the collective wisdom and diverse perspectives within the team, they could refine their approaches and tailor them to meet the needs of their students better.

Full staff learning sessions provided another platform for educators to share their practices and insights. These meetings became forums for lively discussions on fostering optimism, promoting a growth mindset, and nurturing unwavering determination in students. The educators celebrated each other's successes and learned from one another's experiences, creating a supportive and collaborative atmosphere.

Outside formal meetings, the educators continued to engage in informal conversations and exchanges. In the staff lounge, during lunch breaks, or in passing in the hallways, they shared stories of triumphs and challenges, seeking advice and offering encouragement. This informal sharing of strategies further strengthened the sense of community and collective responsibility for fostering optimism and hope.

The expectation of sharing extended beyond just the educators themselves; it was embedded in the culture of the Si Se Puede Pre-K-12 school district. Administrators, instructional coaches, and other support staff actively participated in these conversations, sharing their expertise and insights. The school community recognized that collaborating and sharing could create a robust student support network.

Through this continuous sharing and collaboration, the educators of the Si Se Puede Pre-K-12 school district created a culture of innovation and growth. They understood that by coming together, learning from one another, and supporting each other, they could collectively empower their students to embrace optimism and hope. It was not just an expectation but a way of being that fueled their mission to create a bright future for every student in their care.

The habit of optimism plays a crucial role in the development of students at all levels of education, from elementary to middle school and high school. Optimism is maintaining a positive mindset, seeing opportunities in challenges, and persevering with a hopeful outlook.

Examples:

- Incorporate gratitude exercises to help students focus on the positive aspects of their lives.
- Share stories of famous individuals who overcame obstacles and achieved success.
- Help students reframe setbacks as opportunities for growth and learning.
- Encourage reflection on failures and mistakes, highlighting the lessons that can be gained from them.
- Guide students to set realistic goals and track their progress.
- Assist students in developing action plans and strategies to achieve their goals.
- Encourage students to envision their future aspirations and the steps required.
- Incorporate discussions and activities that explore the power of positive thinking and its impact on their success.

Fostering optimism in students of all levels involves providing them with tools and strategies to reframe challenges, appreciate their strengths, and persist with a positive mindset. By instilling this habit, educators empower students to face obstacles confidently, adapt to change, and maintain hope for a bright future.

Thought Spark Questions: Optimism

1. How can we intentionally cultivate a classroom environment that promotes and nurtures the attitude of optimism among our students?

2. What strategies or activities can we incorporate to help students develop a positive mindset and see opportunities in challenges?

3. How can we encourage students to embrace a hopeful outlook and persist with optimism even when faced with setbacks or obstacles?

4. How can we model and reinforce the importance of positive self-talk and optimistic thinking in our classroom?

5. How can we provide ongoing support and guidance to students in maintaining their optimism and belief in their abilities throughout their educational journey?

Chapter 4 Conclusion

This chapter's primary focus has been on providing teachers and students with the strategies and attributes (also known as superpowers) to make advanced academic experiences the norm in schools. It is essential to recognize that all students desire engagement and challenge. To nurture each student's unique strengths, passions, and talents, we must embrace and incorporate the strategies, skills, and habits discussed in this chapter into our daily school routines.

If someone asked me to summarize this chapter, it's about expectations, beliefs, competence, and confidence. To ensure students succeed in curriculum and experiences traditionally reserved for students with the gifted label, we need to have the competence to provide those opportunities. By acquiring our own "superpowers" as educators and providing "superpowers" to students, I truly believe we gain the confidence to make it work. And yet, we can give teachers the strategies, skills, and supportive culture they need to empower students with these habits, skills, and behaviors; and still there will often be some people who may doubt whether this can be achieved.

The next chapter, Chapter 5, focuses on resistance and inspiration. It's important to note that resistance is neither good nor bad; it simply exists. People have logical and illogical reasons for resisting change, and we must address both. But alongside resistance, we can find inspiration in the success of others.

In the second part of Chapter 5, we will explore several school districts that have embraced the idea of nurturing each student's unique strengths, passions, and talents. These districts, their schools, and the teacher teams within them will serve as sources of inspiration. Additionally, I highlight the stories of individuals who have become true inspirations by embodying these superpowers. These powerful narratives will illustrate how essential behaviors, skills, attitudes, and habits can positively impact students' lives. By showcasing these stories, we affirm that every student can cultivate these attributes, become confident and competent individuals, and excel academically while pursuing their passions. Their strengths become their gift, both to themselves and to the world.

CHAPTER 5

R = Resistance & Inspiration

"What I know today does not make yesterday wrong;
it makes tomorrow better."
—Vanessa Lonster[129]

CHANGE

I usually embrace change. However, during the early months of 2020, around February and March, I grappled with a wave of anxiety. The regular rhythm of extensive travel and global presentations, to which I had grown accustomed, abruptly halted due to the pandemic. This sudden loss of control shook me, and the transition from frequent travel to staying home proved to be a significant challenge. In this new setting, I resisted change intensely, feeling as though I was frozen, much like a deer caught in headlights.

This resistance was fueled by the overarching uncertainty that enveloped us. As we collectively tried to make sense of the global upheaval, I confronted a sense of losing my identity and strength tied to the work I was familiar with. The idea of redefining myself as a consultant and educator, offering support to teams in different districts, felt overwhelming, resulting in an extended period of feeling stuck.

Nonetheless, as time progressed, I realized that the substantial change I was navigating was not my struggle alone. The entire world

129. Lonster, Vanessa, *What I Learn Today Doesn't Make Yesterday Wrong; It Makes Tomorrow Better*, Amazon Digital Services, 2019.

was grappling with similar challenges. This awareness prompted me to trust that emerging from this challenging period would result in collective strength and wisdom, where we would be better equipped to tackle future hurdles. Although this form of change differed from the shifts encountered in educational contexts—such as new curricula, policies, programs, procedures, and new leadership—the fundamental principle remained constant: understanding the underlying reason for change was pivotal. Equipped with tools to navigate this transformation and fortified by trust in the process, I took proactive measures to embrace and manage change.

Whether we're discussing modifications to personal habits or orchestrating a complete overhaul of an organizational culture, the concept of change can prove to be quite daunting. People often exhibit a tendency to oppose change in various domains, and this resistance stems from a range of factors. One significant factor is the apprehension of the unknown. When change enters the scene, it disrupts our accustomed routines and introduces an element of uncertainty, which can spark anxiety and resistance. Our natural inclination is to seek stability and predictability because that's where we find comfort.

Dr. Dennis O'Grady aptly stated: "Change often has a negative reputation in our society. However, it's not all negative—in reality. Change is a vital part of life—it propels us forward, fuels growth, and maintains our engagement. Imagine a life devoid of change; it would be stagnant, monotonous, and uninspiring."[130] This underscores the indispensable role of change in our lives and underscores the necessity of embracing its transformative potential.

Logical vs. Illogical Resistance to Change

In their book *Time for Change: 4 Essential Skills for Transformational School and District Leaders*, authors Anthony Muhammad and

---

130. "20 Transformational Quotes on Change Management," TopRight, https://toprightpartners.com/insights/20-transformational-quotes-on-change-management.

Luis Cruz highlight four fundamental skills leaders must possess to transform educational settings. These skills are helping stakeholders understand *why* the change is needed, creating trusting relationships, being transparent and sharing leadership responsibilities (the *who*), providing the proper time support and training to accomplish what is being asked (the *how*), and expecting the work to be accomplished (the *do*).[131]

The first skill, understanding why, emphasizes the importance of leaders having a clear and compelling vision for change. Leaders must articulate why change is necessary and communicate it effectively to all stakeholders. By establishing a shared understanding of the purpose and direction of change, leaders inspire motivation and commitment among their team members.

Creating trusting relationships is the second skill emphasized in the book. Transformational leaders understand that trust is the foundation of effective collaboration and growth. They invest time and effort in building relationships based on respect, authenticity, and open communication. By fostering trust, leaders create an environment where individuals can take risks, share ideas, and work together toward common goals.

The third skill highlighted is providing support and training around *how*. Leaders recognize that for change to occur, individuals need the necessary knowledge, skills, and resources. They proactively provide support through professional learning opportunities, mentorship programs, and ongoing coaching. By equipping their team members with the tools and guidance they need, leaders empower them to implement change strategies effectively.

The fourth and final skill is expecting production because they have taken the time to provide the members of the organization with the first three levels of support, giving them the why, the who, and the how. Transformational leaders set high expectations for performance and hold themselves and their team members accountable. They create a

131. Muhammad, Anthony and Cruz, Luis. *Time for Change: 4 Essential Skills for Transformational School and District Leaders*, Solution Tree Press, 2019.

culture of excellence and continuous improvement, motivating individuals to achieve their best. Leaders foster a productive and results-oriented environment by setting clear goals, providing regular feedback, and celebrating successes.

In summary, the book *Time for Change* underscores the significance of understanding *why*, creating trusting relationships (who), providing support and training around *how*, and expecting production(do) as essential skills for transformational school and district leaders. By cultivating these skills, leaders can drive meaningful change, nurture everyone's unique strengths, and create a positive and productive educational environment.

Cruz and Muhammad say it's unethical to start with the *do* as it will breed compliance instead of commitment. Leaders must use the first three tools, the *why*, *who*, and *how* to engage educators in committing to *do* the work or make the necessary changes. If leaders have taken the time to support educators with the first three tools and some people resist, they must use the positional power to insist that they comply with the group's will. They must closely monitor those individuals to ensure they engage and do the work.

MOVING FORWARD

Here's a Story...The Innov8 District

In the **Innov8 District**, Superintendent Dr. Mike Durso introduced the possibility of implementing standards-based grading in elementary schools. However, the idea encountered both logical and illogical resistance from various stakeholders.

The logical resistance stemmed from some individuals who did not understand the *why* behind the change. They questioned the need for a shift in grading practices and sought clarity on how standards-based grading would benefit students.

Additionally, there were concerns about trust due to previous experiences with a top-down leadership style from the previous superintendent. Some community members feared this change would be another directive imposed without their input or consideration.

On the other hand, illogical resistance came from a group of individuals who resisted change because they preferred to stick with traditional grading methods. Their resistance was rooted in a desire to maintain the status quo, even if it may not be the most effective approach for student learning and growth.

Superintendent Durso and the school leaders took a strategic and collaborative approach to address these different forms of resistance. They organized town hall meetings and open forums to explain the rationale behind standards-based grading comprehensively. They shared research and evidence demonstrating the positive impact of this approach on student achievement and equitable assessment. Dr. Durso encouraged open dialogue, patiently answering questions, and addressing concerns while actively listening to the perspectives of the community.

To build trust and overcome skepticism, Dr. Durso and the school leaders made a concerted effort to involve stakeholders in the decision-making process. They formed committees consisting of parents, teachers, administrators, and community members to collaboratively explore the implementation of standards-based grading. This inclusive approach gave everyone a voice and actively participated in shaping the new grading system.

Recognizing the need for training and support, the district provided extensive professional learning opportunities. Teachers received comprehensive training on standards-based grading, including workshops, seminars, and coaching sessions. Instructional coaches and experienced educators served as mentors, guiding their colleagues through the transition, sharing effective practices, and addressing individual concerns.

Over time, teachers gained a deeper understanding of standards-based grading and witnessed its positive impact on student learning. Only a few staff continued to resist. Dr. Durso and the other school leaders closely monitored those who resisted and said they would do so until they willingly complied. Over time most of this illogical resistance began to dissipate. The collaborative efforts and ongoing support helped teachers overcome their fears and develop confidence in implementing the new grading system effectively. As the educators embraced the change and experienced success, their enthusiasm and positive results became evident to the community.

Superintendent Durso and the school leaders addressed the logical and illogical resistance to standards-based grading through transparent communication, collaboration, and providing the necessary support and training. Their efforts ensured that all stakeholders understood the purpose and benefits of this change, and gradually, the entire community rallied behind the transformation, paving the way for successful implementation and improved educational experiences for the students of Innov8 School District.

Thought Spark Questions:

1. How might the principles of standards-based grading and the strategies used by Superintendent Durso and the school leaders apply to the broader concept of gifted education for all students, transcending labels? Consider how transparent communication, collaborative decision-making, and providing adequate support could help overcome resistance and misconceptions about the benefits of gifted education for all.

2. In the context of making gifted education the floor for all students, what examples of logical resistance could arise, and how might these individuals misunderstand the underlying reasons for the change? How

would you address their concerns and help them grasp the importance of providing advanced education opportunities for all learners?

3. Just as stakeholders in the story sought clarity on the benefits of standards-based grading, how might you articulate the advantages of an inclusive approach to gifted education? How would you engage parents, teachers, and the community to ensure they understand the potential positive impact on students and the overall learning environment?

4. Consider the illogical resistance faced by those who clung to traditional grading methods. How could a similar mindset hinder the implementation of gifted education for all? How would you navigate these attitudes and help individuals recognize the broader advantages of fostering talent and unlimited potential for all students?

5. Drawing parallels between Superintendent Durso's strategies and the implementation of gifted education for all, how might you address the illogical resistance from those who might resist change due to personal preferences? What strategies would you employ to emphasize the educational benefits and overcome resistance to transforming the system?

6. Reflecting on the four essential skills from *Time for Change*, how could these skills be adapted to promote gifted education for all students? How might understanding the purpose, building relationships, providing necessary training, and setting expectations contribute to successfully shifting the education paradigm?

7. In the context of implementing gifted education for all, how could collaboration and shared decision-making among stakeholders help address resistance? How might involving teachers, parents, and students themselves in the decision-making process lead to a more inclusive and effective educational approach?

8. How can the experiences and strategies highlighted in the story of the **Innov8 District** serve as a guide for addressing resistance and driving change in your efforts to provide gifted education for all students? How could you apply these lessons to create a more inclusive and equitable educational environment in your school or district?

Finding Inspiration in the Success of Others

During my time as the principal of Mount Eagle Elementary School, we were working hard to make progress. At the same time, some of our staff had doubts about whether we could do this for all students. That's when I reached out to my mentor, Lillie Jessie, who was a highly respected principal in a nearby school district. Her school was like ours but twice as big, and they were doing amazing things on behalf of their students. Every staff member there was working as a team to help all the students succeed.

These visits were pivotal moments for us. We decided to visit Lillie's school twice, with half of our staff going each time. These visits had a big impact. They showed us that our goals were possible. Seeing what Lillie's school had achieved made us believe that we could do it too.

Getting inspired by others' success is a strong force for making ourselves better. When we see someone else achieve something great, it can make us want to improve ourselves too. It's like a spark that pushes us to aim higher.

Learning from other people's success is important too. We can see different ways, methods, and attitudes that lead to good results. By studying how successful people did it, we can learn what skills and habits helped them succeed.

Also, seeing others succeed can make us believe in our own abilities. It shows us that we can reach our goals if we work hard. When we see others do it, it gives us motivation to set high standards for ourselves and try our best.

Being inspired by others' success is a positive way of thinking. Instead of feeling jealous or thinking there's not enough success to go around, we can see it as a team effort. We realize that success is something everyone can achieve, and by celebrating others' achievements, we create a good atmosphere for everyone.

Looking up to others' success can also make us more ambitious. We can find role models who guide us and give us advice. Their stories of overcoming challenges can inspire us to keep going, even when things are tough.

Finding motivation from others' success can be a big deal. It makes us want to do better, makes us believe in our own unlimited potential, and drives us to succeed. When we look at others' achievements with respect, curiosity, and a desire to learn, we create a space where we can grow personally and understand that we too can achieve greatness.

Inspirational School Districts

Inspiration in Iowa, Clear Lake Community District Schools

DOUG GEE, SUPERINTENDENT

Clear Lake School District in Iowa is renowned for nurturing students' unique strengths, passions, and talents. With a focus on providing high-quality education that celebrates each student, the district has established itself as a beacon of educational excellence.

The Clear Lake Administrative Team has been instrumental in shaping the district's vision and implementing innovative programs to support students' holistic development. Recognizing the importance of fostering creativity and encouraging students to explore their passions, Gee has led initiatives to provide diverse learning opportunities for all students within the district.

One of the district's notable initiatives is the integration of Project Lead The Way (PLTW) programs. By incorporating PLTW's hands-on learning experiences in science, technology, engineering, and mathematics (STEM), Clear Lake School District enables students to engage in real-world projects and problem-solving. This approach cultivates their interest in STEM and enhances their critical thinking and collaboration skills. Superintendent Gee and his team have championed the expansion of PLTW, recognizing its impact on preparing students for the rapidly evolving demands of the twenty-first century.

In addition to PLTW, Clear Lake School District strongly emphasizes social-emotional learning (SEL). The Clear Lake Administrative Team has worked diligently to create a nurturing and inclusive environment where students feel supported and valued. SEL skills, such as empathy, resilience, and teamwork, are integrated into the curriculum, helping students develop emotional intelligence and interpersonal skills vital for personal and academic success.

The Clear Lake Administrative Team understands the importance of extracurricular activities in fostering students' unique talents and passions. Clear Lake School District offers a wide range of opportunities beyond the classroom, including art clubs, music ensembles, theater programs, and sports teams. These extracurricular activities allow students to explore their interests, develop their skills, and pursue their passions in a supportive and encouraging environment.

Teachers within Clear Lake School District also play a pivotal role in nurturing students' individuality. The Clear Lake Administrative Team has prioritized ongoing professional learning for educators, ensuring they are equipped with the latest best practices in education. This investment empowers teachers to create engaging and personalized learning experiences tailored to students' unique strengths and learning styles. As mentors, teachers guide students in discovering and developing their talents, instilling in them a sense of purpose and self-confidence.

Clear Lake School District's dedication to nurturing each student's unique strengths, passions, and talents has garnered attention and recognition from other educational institutions. Educators from different districts visit Clear Lake to learn about the district's success and innovative approaches. The district's philosophy of providing a gifted education to every student, regardless of academic standing, has transformed the educational landscape and created an inclusive environment where every student can thrive.

As students progress through middle and high school in Clear Lake, the district continues to provide opportunities for them to explore their passions further. Advanced courses and specialized programs in various disciplines, such as advanced sciences, fine arts, and vocational education, enable students to pursue their interests at a higher level, preparing them for future success in their chosen fields.

Under the leadership of Superintendent Doug Gee, Clear Lake School District has become a beacon of educational excellence, dedicated to nurturing each student's unique strengths, passions, and talents. With an unwavering commitment to personalized learning, innovative programs, and a supportive environment, the district prepares students for a future where their individuality and diverse talents are celebrated and valued. The transformative impact of Superintendent Gee's leadership has solidified Clear Lake School District's reputation as a model for educational institutions striving to create a nurturing and inclusive environment for all students.[132]

Every Child, in Every School, Every Day in Kildeer Countryside CCSD 96

BY JULIE SCHMIDT, FORMER SUPERINTENDENT

As the recently retired Superintendent of Kildeer Countryside CCSD 96, I am excited to share how our district's mission, vision, beliefs, actions, and practices align with the core principles outlined in this book.

---

132. Gee, Doug, "Inspiration in Iowa—Clear Lake Community District Schools, personal communication (interview), June 2023.

Our mission statement is clear: to ensure every student reaches his or her maximum potential. However, it is essential to note that we cautiously approach the concept of maximum potential. We firmly believe that no individual or team has the right to predetermine any student's maximum potential. We reject that potential is determined solely by test scores, previous performance, or background. Instead, we are committed to creating an inclusive and supportive environment where all students thrive.

Our vision is to become the premier elementary school district in the nation. This vision serves as a guiding light for us, especially during challenging times like the pandemic. We constantly ask ourselves, "What would a premier school district do?" when making decisions regarding resource allocation and navigating unprecedented challenges.

When defining high levels of learning in our district, we acknowledge that it extends beyond grade-level expectations. While we strive for grade-level proficiency or beyond, we understand the importance of not predefining high levels for individual students. We recognize that each student has unique strengths, passions, and talents and are committed to tailoring our support and instruction accordingly.

Regarding the book's title, *Every Student Deserves a Gifted Education*, our district fully embraces this belief. We have moved away from the traditional model of identifying a small group of students based on test scores and pulling them out of their classrooms for more rigorous learning. We realized that this model was not serving our students effectively and did not align with our mission, vision, or values.

Under the visionary leadership of Dr. Tom Many, we began reshaping the role of our "Gifted" teachers to be part of the instructional coaching team. Their primary focus became supporting all teachers in developing and implementing extension opportunities for all students across all grade levels and subjects. This shift allowed us to provide daily and unit-by-unit extension and enrichment for all students.

When our state adopted new, more rigorous standards, we took immediate action. We prioritized and unpacked these standards, clarifying the rigor required for each target. In our system, this is referred to as a 3.0 target. Additionally, we employed a taxonomy approach to identify a 4.0 extension target for every extendable target. These 4.0 targets seamlessly became part of our rubrics, assignments, assessments, and reporting system. Every student in our district can access the 4.0 target as they are ready.

To illustrate the impact of our approach, let me share a heartwarming story. On a rainy Monday morning, I spontaneously entered a first-grade classroom through the back door of one of our elementary schools. The students were deeply engaged, taking a pre-assessment as they were about to start a new unit. Curious, I approached a first-grade boy and asked him what he was doing. His eyes lit up with enthusiasm as he replied, "I'm taking a pre-assessment!" Intrigued, I inquired further, "Why are you doing that?" Without hesitation, he confidently responded, "If I don't do a pre-assessment, how will my teacher know what I already know?!" Several hours later, I was drawn back to the same classroom as I was leaving. To my delight, I discovered that the same student was deeply engaged in reviewing the results of the pre-assessment, using a rubric to set a goal for the upcoming unit. When asked about his current task, he eagerly exclaimed, "Remember that pre-assessment? I am currently at a 2.0 but set a goal to reach a 4.0!" This particular student, who happened to be entitled to special education services, exemplified the power of our approach.

Beyond the 4.0 targets present at every grade level and in every subject, we also develop Individualized Learning Plans (ILPs) to address the unique needs of some students. These plans may include acceleration when appropriate, ensuring that each student's learning journey is tailored to their specific requirements.

Below is an example of what that might look like.

Target	4.0 Extends	3.5	3.0 Mastery	2.5	2.0 Developing	1.5	1.0 Not Mastering
4.NBT.2 Read and write multi-digit whole numbers using base-ten numerals, number names, and expanded form. Compare two multi-digit numbers based on meanings of the digits in each place, >, =, and < symbols to record the results of comparisons.	Solve multi-step problems to compare whole numbers up to 1,000,000 in digits using base-ten numerals, number names, and expanded form. Develop a logical argument to justify the selection of the best response. **Demonstrated by:** Students using one comparison statement to compare three whole number (using two symbols). Explanation should showcase an understanding of place value using precise mathematical vocabulary.		**Strong** conceptual understanding of whole numbers using base-ten numerals, number names, and expanded forms, and comparing two multi-digit numbers. **Demonstrated by:** Ability to read and write whole numbers using base-ten numerals, number names, **AND** expanded form. **AND** Use symbols to compare whole numbers.		**Inconsistent** conceptual understanding of whole numbers using base-ten numerals, number names, and expanded forms, and comparing two multi-digit numbers. **Demonstrated by:** Ability to read and write whole numbers using base-ten numerals, number names, and/or expanded form. **AND** Use symbols to compare whole numbers. **AND** Student is successful with teacher scaffolds and support.		**Lack of** conceptual understanding of whole numbers using base-ten numerals, number names, and expanded forms, and comparing two multi-digit numbers. **Demonstrated by:** High levels of scaffolds and support.

Below is an example of data when **4.0** targets are included on all Common Formative Assessments (CFAs) and unit assessments.

Sample Data Collection Google Doc

Learning Standard Lit 3.6 Distinguish their own point of view from that of the narrator or those of the characters.	Informal CFA Check-In 1 Ticket in	Informal CFA Check-In 2 Group Ob	More Formal Check-In 3 CFA	Informal CFA Check-In 4 Ticket Out	Informal CFA Check-In 5 Unit Assess
TEACHER A—Aimee (25)					
4.0 Extends	2	2	5	5	8
3.0–3.5 Mastery	8	12	15	17	16
2.0–2.5 Developing Mastery	13	10	5	3	1
1.0–1.5 Not Mastering	4	1			
					80%
TEACHER B—Jenny (23)					
4.0 Extends	3	4	5	5	10
3.0–3.5 Mastery	9	10	12	14	9
2.0–2.5 Developing Mastery	6	5	4	2	3
1.0–1.5 Not Mastering	5	4	2	1	
					74%
TEACHER C—Jane (26)					
4.0 Extends	8	9	8	7	10
3.0–3.5 Mastery	12	12	11	14	14
2.0–2.5 Developing Mastery	5	4	7	5	2
1.0–1.5 Not Mastering	1	1			
					73%

Regarding the fallacy of fixed intelligence, we have taken decisive action. We recognized inappropriate assessments perpetuating a fixed intelligence mindset, such as the Cognitive Abilities Test (Cogat). We committed to eliminating such assessments and increasing levels of student engagement. We strive to create an environment where all students feel seen and heard in the classroom, fostering a growth mindset and an understanding that intelligence is not fixed but can be developed.

Our district has made significant strides that align with the core principles outlined in this book. We believe that all children have gifts, and our actions and practices reflect this belief. We have implemented the necessary shifts to nurture the unique strengths, passions, and talents of each student, providing access and opportunities for all students to discover their untapped potential and pursue their passions.[133]

Final Insight on Kildeer

Tom Manning, Julie Schmidt, Jeanne Spiller, and the rest of the staff in Kildeer exemplify the courage it takes to challenge the conventional notion of gifted education, which was previously reserved for a select few. Instead, they champion the idea of providing gifted education for all students.

Mineola Grows—Mineola School District, NY
Empowering Learners to Understand Their Brain and Embracing the Growth Mindset

DR. MICHAEL NAGLER, SUPERINTENDENT

"Mineola Grows" is an innovative online video initiative produced by Mineola School District, conceived initially to empower learners within their community. However, its impact has transcended the boundaries of the Mineola School District, gaining nationwide recognition and widespread use by educators.

---

133. Schmidt, Julie, "Every Child, in Every School, Every Day in Kildeer—Kildeer Countryside CCSD 96," personal communication (interview), June 2023.

Led by the visionary leadership of Dr. Michael Nagler, superintendent of Mineola School District, Mineola Grows harnesses the power of neuroscience and growth mindset principles to transform learning environments.

Mineola Grows provides comprehensive resources designed to empower educators and students alike. In-classroom activities and targeted video lessons equip educators with the tools to create an inclusive and empowering learning environment. These resources are built upon a foundation of over a decade of research into growth mindset best practices, ensuring they are practical and impactful.

While initially intended for learners within Mineola School District, Mineola Grows has resonated with educators nationwide. Its video series covers various neuroscience and growth mindset topics, including "Meet Your Brain," "Your Neurons," "Activate Your Neurons," "Dr. Nagler's Laboratory," and much more. These videos serve as invaluable resources for professional learning, offering guidance and support to educators seeking to enhance their understanding of the brain and incorporate growth mindset practices into their classrooms.

The impact of Mineola Grows extends beyond educators. Students and parents have also reaped this transformative initiative's benefits. Through accessible and engaging video content, students gain a deeper understanding of their brain functions and how they relate to their learning experiences. With neuroscience insights, parents are better equipped to support their children's growth mindset development, fostering a home environment that reinforces the principles embraced in the Mineola Grows project.

The success and widespread use of Mineola Grows is a testament to the power of accessible educational resources in promoting a growth mindset and transforming learning experiences. Mineola School District's commitment to nurturing learners extends beyond their community, positively impacting educators, students, and parents nationwide. Dr. Nagler credits the expertise of district instructional leader Jennifer Maichin and videographer Stephen Interrante in creating age-appropriate, engaging videos to tackle the complex science related to our brains. Because of the forward-thinking leadership of Dr. Michael Nagler and his team, Mineola Grows continues to inspire learners across the country, empowering them to embrace their unlimited potential and embark on a lifelong journey of growth, optimism, and discovery.[134]

Nurturing Curiosity
Greenfield Union School District's Journey to Unleashing the Genius Within Each Student

ZANDRA GALVÁN, SUPERINTENDENT, GREENFIELD, CALIFORNIA

"We want to make sure that, whatever we do, we do it on a large scale, so every student has that experience."

—SUPERINTENDENT ZANDRA JO GALVÁN

Amidst the sprawling landscapes of Greenfield, California, a beacon of educational innovation and inclusivity shines brightly within the community—the Greenfield Union School District. At its helm is its visionary leader, Superintendent Zandra Jo Galván, whose passion for cultivating curiosity has ignited a transformative journey of nurturing each student's unique strengths, passions, and talents.

The district's commitment to fostering curiosity as a cornerstone of its educational philosophy is a testament to its dedication to unlocking the hidden genius within every learner. Superintendent Galván and her team have strategically woven the attribute of curiosity into the very fabric of the district's approach, recognizing it as a powerful catalyst for sparking engagement, creativity, and a lifelong love of learning.

---

134. Nagler, Michael, "Mineola Grows—Empowering Learners to Understand Their Brain and Embracing the Growth Mindset," personal communication (interview), June 2023.

Central to this endeavor is the understanding that curiosity is not a mere fleeting moment of wonder but a driving force that propels students toward deeper exploration and understanding. With an unwavering belief that "ALL means ALL," the district ensures that every student, regardless of their background or circumstances, can embark on a journey of intellectual discovery.

The district's commitment to curiosity-driven education is reflected in its collaborative ethos, where educators, students, and families join hands to create an ecosystem that nurtures inquisitiveness. This collaborative spirit is not confined to the classroom alone but extends to the very heart of the community. Superintendent Galván envisions a network of support that embraces open dialogue, encourages idea-sharing, and fosters an environment where questions are celebrated as precursors to innovation.

Innovative teaching methodologies and immersive learning experiences are the foundation for the district's curiosity-centric approach. The curriculum is designed to kindle the flames of inquiry, with hands-on projects, interactive learning tools, and real-world applications at its core. Students are encouraged to delve into subjects that resonate with their interests, guided by the belief that curiosity is the compass that points the way toward one's passions.

One groundbreaking embodiment of this philosophy is the district's strategic partnership with LEGO Education and Apple. This alliance has ushered in a new era of experiential learning, amplifying the power of curiosity. Through the FIRST LEGO League, every Pre-K-6 student in the district experiences the thrill of hands-on exploration. These young minds, ignited by the spark of curiosity, now find themselves immersed in STEM, where creativity, critical thinking, and collaboration converge.

Apple's innovative contributions, from cutting-edge technology to enriching professional development, further enhance the district's commitment to curiosity. Student-centered LEGO and Apple learning spaces have become exploration hubs where students learn about technology and actively harness it to unravel their unique genius.

Despite unprecedented challenges, such as the recent global pandemic, Superintendent Galván's resolve remains unshaken. The district's commitment to fostering curiosity, fortified by its partnership with LEGO Education and Apple, has proven to be a guiding light during these trying times. Through virtual learning initiatives, creative remote projects, and a seamless transition to digital platforms, the district continues to fuel the flames of curiosity, ensuring that every student's innate genius continues to flourish.

In the nurturing embrace of Greenfield Union School District, curiosity is not just an attribute but a way of life. It is an invitation to explore, question, and uncover the unlimited potential that lies within each student. Superintendent Galván's visionary leadership, combined with the transformative partnership with LEGO Education and Apple, has created a thriving school district where curiosity is celebrated and cherished as the driving force behind a future where the possibilities are endless.[135]

These four districts stand as beacons of inspiration in a landscape of educational excellence. Guided by visionary leaders, Clear Lake Community District Schools, Mineola School District, Greenfield Union School District, and Kildeer Countryside CCSD 96 have redefined education, nurturing each student's unique strengths, passions, and talents. Through their unwavering commitment, they illuminate a path toward a future where unlimited potential and gifted educational experiences become the floor of every classroom.

Personal Stories of Inspiration

These personal stories of inspiration emphasize the common humanity we all share. They depict ordinary individuals who embrace the attributes of the seven essential behavior skills, attitudes, and habits known

135. Galván, Zandra. "Nurturing the Genius Within Each Student—Greenfield Union School District, Greenfield, California," personal communication (interview), June 2023.

as student superpowers to nurture their unique strengths, passions, and talents. These individuals embody persistence, precise thinking, effective communication, self-control, empathy, curiosity, flexible thinking, and optimism. Marguarite Gooden, Andrew Mallon, Calvin Barnes, and Carolina Aguiar are examples of countless individuals who have demonstrated these attributes and should resonate with people from all walks of life, including yourselves.

Marguarite Gooden

A STORY OF PASSION, PERSEVERANCE, AND SHEDDING PERCEPTIONS

Marguarite Gooden, a dedicated and passionate now retired educator, embarked on a journey that showcased the transformative power of belief in students, advocacy for the underserved, and the courage to challenge societal norms. Her story unfolded in Arlington, Virginia, during the 1950s, a time of racial segregation and adversity.

Growing up in Halls Hill, one of the three all-Black neighborhoods in Arlington, Marguarite came from a family with a remarkable history. Her maternal great-grandparents were freed enslaved people from the Basil Hall plantation, which eventually became Halls Hill. Her maternal great-grandmother even had the distinction of being a teacher and a friend of Frederick Douglass. Despite facing numerous challenges, Margarite's parents were professionals in their respective fields. Her father, one of the original firefighters at Station 8, shattered barriers as the first Black paid firefighter below the Mason-Dixon Line.

In her close-knit community, Marguarite experienced a joyful childhood, despite the limitations imposed by the Jim Crow era. Her parents ensured she and her siblings were exposed to cultural experiences beyond their neighborhood, visiting restaurants, movies, theaters, and museums in Washington, D.C. They even traveled to St. Vincent, her paternal grandmother's birthplace in the West Indies.

Marguarite's educational journey began at Langston Elementary, an all-Black school known for its outstanding teachers who were deeply connected to their communities. Marguarite cherished the familiarity of seeing her teachers at church and local events. In 1959, four students from Langston integrated Stratford Junior High School, marking a significant milestone for Virginia. Four years later, Marguarite's sixth-grade class joined them at Stratford. However, being the only Black student in her classes presented immense challenges. At Langston, Marguarite was an A-B honor roll student, but once she went to Stratford she was a C student and received her first D on her report card. She faced discrimination and ignorance, enduring hurtful comments questioning her race, such as being asked if she had a tail by some girls. Initially, her academic performance suffered, and she was told that she was only reading at a third-grade level. Nevertheless, her parents consistently encouraged her to stay focused, emphasizing that her true value lay in her knowledge and abilities.

In 1966 Marguarite entered Yorktown High School, one of the two schools gerrymandered for integration. Being the sole Black student in the tenth grade initially overwhelmed her, leading her to cry daily before school. Some of her classmates exhibited hostility, including harassment from the son of a KKK wizard. However, Marguarite's parents swiftly met with the principal and demanded a resolution. The boys were removed from her class, and her teacher reassured her unwavering support.

Despite her adversities, Marguarite encountered remarkable teachers in high school who inspired her to pursue her dream of becoming an educator. She developed lifelong connections with them and formed friendships during her senior year. These experiences shaped her character and fueled her determination to make a difference in the lives of marginalized students.

Marguarite began her college journey at Hofstra University in Long Island, New York, but later transferred to Morgan State University in Baltimore, Maryland. In 1975, she graduated from Morgan with a BA in Elementary Education. Though her initial SAT scores indicated slim chances of success in college, Marguarite refused to let standardized tests define her abilities. She later pursued a master's in education administration from George Mason University.

Marguarite's passion for education stemmed from her childhood experiences, when she witnessed the scarcity of teachers who resembled her. She yearned to help underserved students and advocate for those often overlooked. As an educator, Marguarite's leadership at New Directions showcased an incredible program that provided second chances to students. She recognized the strengths these students brought to the table—creative thinking, effective communication skills, and natural leadership qualities.

Despite her students' adverse childhood experiences, Marguarite firmly believed they could achieve anything with the appropriate opportunities and support. She refused to lower the bar for her students, rejecting the negative labels they had been burdened with. Instead, she empowered them to see their true unlimited potential and believe in the positive aspects of themselves.

Marguarite acknowledged that traditional thinking and mindsets surrounding giftedness had hindered progress in education. She understood it was easy to cling to outdated beliefs and blame students when things didn't go as planned. However, Marguarite believed that it took hard work, dedication, and a commitment to understanding each student individually to meet their unique needs and help them succeed.

Marguarite's unwavering belief in the worth of each student fueled her passion for fighting on behalf of those who had been given up on. She championed the "No Child Left Behind" notion and tirelessly worked to make it a reality. With perseverance, courage, and the support of a dedicated staff who shared her vision, Marguarite never gave up on her students. In turn, her students began to believe in themselves.

Marguarite's journey as an educator exemplified the transformative power of believing in students, advocating for the underserved, and challenging the status quo. Through her unwavering dedication, she made a lasting impact on the lives of countless individuals, proving that with the proper support and opportunities, every child can thrive and succeed.[136]

Andrew Mallon

"We feared that Andrew might skip school or even drop out without the incentive of the carpentry class to keep him engaged."

—JOHN AND SANDY MALLON, ANDREW'S PARENTS[137]

FROM POTENTIAL HIGH SCHOOL DROPOUT TO WORLD-CLASS TREE SCULPTOR

In His Own Words

As I started kindergarten, full of energy and intrigue, I didn't know what I was good or bad at. In first grade, I had my special reading class, one-on-one with the teacher. My teachers and parents also told me I had trouble reading and writing. My older brother and sister had similar difficulties and recognized the signs early on. I'm unsure if being told I wasn't good at something at such a young age helped or hurt me before I fully understood it. It made me self-conscious about school. However, I still had a passion driving me—the passion to do what I enjoyed. What I enjoyed was creating things I could see and imagine.

Art projects were my favorite activities. My art projects were always far better than those of my peers. I vividly remember a first-grade project where we had to build a space shuttle. I knew the shapes and proportions of a space shuttle from images, and I was able to find materials that would create a space shuttle with proper proportions (I

---

136. Gooden, Marguarite, "A Story of Passion, Perseverance, and Shedding Perceptions," Personal communication (interview), July 2023.

137. Mallon, Sandy and Mallon, John, personal communication (interview), July 2023.

wish I still had that space shuttle). I asked my mother why the other kids' projects didn't look like space shuttles while mine was so good. She told me that we all have different things we are good at. My struggles with reading and my amazing art projects continued throughout primary school. I always needed extra help with my classwork, but I excelled at my art projects.

As I progressed through middle and high school, my reading and writing abilities became even greater obstacles for me, and there were fewer and fewer art projects. The struggles intensified. This made me realize strongly that I couldn't do anything. I had to find my path based on my strengths. Since I enjoyed building things, that's where I focused my attention. I took shop classes in middle school and high school. I loved watching home remodeling television shows. I built whatever I could in my basement, using whatever wood and tools I could find. I constructed tree forts with my friends. I wanted to take a sculpture class in high school but couldn't because I had to take an extra study hall class. My mother had to fight to get me into the carpentry class when my schedule didn't have room for it because she knew it was what I needed to succeed. I excelled in my carpentry class throughout high school, and my carpentry teacher even helped me get a job working for his brother's construction company during the summers.

When I graduated from high school, it was a relief not to have any more schoolwork. I could finally do what I loved—creating. Naturally, I excelled at my job as a carpenter. I became the lead carpenter, managing a few older guys under me. I never faced any resentment from my coworkers because they knew I had a strong passion. I loved my career in carpentry. However, I always felt like something was missing. I was always working based on someone else's plans and designs. I needed more.

I needed to express myself from my heart. That's when I discovered hand carving, delicately shaping small pieces of wood into whatever my mind could imagine. Realizing I could create anything I wanted, I still knew I needed to find a way to survive as an artist. With my amazing ability to sculpt and create anything I could imagine, I needed to scale it up and speed up the process. I saw people on TV doing chainsaw carving, and I knew that was for me. I shared my dream of becoming a chainsaw artist with my friends and family, and they encouraged me to take a class to get started. So that's what I did. I returned from class, emptied my change jar, and bought my first chainsaw. That's how my career as a chainsaw artist began. It consumed my thoughts, which made it easy for me to excel. After four years of chainsaw carving on the side, working as a carpenter, I leaped and became a full-time carver. Going full-time only made me faster and better. Soon, my peers recognized me as an amazing artist, and now I am known as one of the top chainsaw carvers in the world.

It's easy to excel at something you were meant for. Literacy continues to be a huge challenge for me but also gives me power as a creator. It's like being blind but having enhanced hearing. My struggles with reading and writing make me a great artist and creator. I believe there are many art forms in which I could excel, but this is the field I chose.

Dealing with my literacy problems is not easy. However, having a good support team around me and utilizing technology make it possible for me to function in life and as a professional business owner.[138]

Nurturing each student's unique strengths, passions, and talents unlocks unlimited potential. Andrew Mallon's journey showcases the transformative power of such support. Despite literacy challenges, his parents and carpentry teacher recognized his talent for woodworking, enabling Andrew to excel in his chosen field and become a renowned chainsaw artist. We empower students to overcome obstacles and realize their boundless capabilities by fostering individual strengths and passions.

Calvin Barnes

A PASSION FOR SPORTS AND SHARING HIS GIFT WITH THE WORLD

Get ready to be inspired by Calvin Barnes, a remarkable individual in the video and television industry whose journey serves as a shining example for educators on the possibilities we can provide to every student based on their interests, strengths, and passions. Calvin's unwavering dedication to his craft and incredible achievements offer invaluable lessons and insights for those committed to nurturing their students' unique talents and interests.

Calvin is making waves in esteemed platforms like TNT and Turner Sports, proving the transformative power of providing students with

---

138. Mallon, Andrew, "From Potential High School Dropout to World-Class Tree Sculptor," personal communication (interview), July 2023.

a variety of opportunities to explore their passions. As a production assistant at Turner Sports, he is actively involved in various TNT and NBA TV shows. From conducting sports research and tracking live game stats to creating captivating graphics and editing videos, Calvin's versatility and commitment to excellence make him an invaluable asset to the TNT crew.

Throughout his journey, Calvin has found inspiration in influential figures like Stuart Scott, Stephen A. Smith, Ernie Johnson, Kevin Harlan, and Mike Breen. These talented individuals breathe life into sports and provide insightful analysis, fueling Calvin's passion for working in video and television. They have left an enduring impact on his career, igniting his desire to bring the excitement of sports to life for fans worldwide. Calvin's high school counselor, John Trusty, also played a pivotal role by introducing him to the world of behind-the-scenes work and guiding him toward his current position.

Calvin's educational trajectory highlights the importance of providing students with many opportunities to explore their passions. While he faced challenges in subjects like chemistry and physics, his resilience, coupled with the support of his parents and classmates, enabled him to overcome these obstacles and achieve academic excellence. Armed with initiative and determination, Calvin conquered subject-related hurdles and emerged victorious.

From a young age, Calvin possessed exceptional skills in presenting and public speaking. His natural ability to confidently engage and captivate audiences set him apart, regardless of the subject matter. This invaluable talent has propelled his career in the video and television industry, where clear and effective communication is paramount. Calvin firmly believes in nurturing fearlessness in the face of failure, encouraging self-expression, and fostering engaging conversations to empower students to thrive in any field.

Calvin's lifelong passion for video and television is rooted in his early morning rituals of waking up to watch ESPN's *SportsCenter*. This commitment to staying well-informed about the previous day's sports events enabled him to actively participate in debates and discussions with his peers. Calvin's unwavering dedication to his interests has significantly influenced his career choices, fueling his desire to work behind the scenes and share the excitement of sports with fans worldwide. He understands that the same dedication and commitment he possessed as a student resonates with aspiring professionals today.

Beyond sharing his journey, Calvin emphasizes giving students many opportunities to discover their passions. He highlights the significance of persistence in overcoming setbacks and challenges that are inevitable in any field. Calvin firmly believes that these experiences teach resilience and empower students to learn and grow from their mistakes.

Furthermore, Calvin champions the vital role of educators in nurturing curiosity and providing platforms for students to express their creativity. By encouraging precise thinking and effective communication, educators can foster a learning environment that equips students with the skills necessary for success. Calvin's experiences also underscore the value of empathy in building meaningful relationships and collaborating with colleagues. He emphasizes the importance of patience, self-control, and understanding as qualities that contribute to a positive and productive atmosphere.

Calvin's remarkable journey demonstrates the transformative impact of offering students diverse opportunities to explore their passions. By providing a nurturing environment and encouraging persistence, curiosity, and empathy, educators can empower their students to discover their unique strengths and interests. Calvin Barnes stands as a beacon of inspiration, lighting the way for educators and students to create a world where everyone can thrive and share their gifts.[139]

Calvin Barnes is the product of P. G. County Public Schools in Maryland and a North Carolina Central University graduate.

---

139. Barnes, Calvin, "A Passion for Sports and Sharing His Gift with the World," personal communication (interview), July 2023.

Carolina Aguiar

A SINGLE MOTHER AND FORMER ENGLISH LANGUAGE LEARNER'S GIFT TO THE WORLD

Embracing Optimism, Persistence, Curiosity, and Self-Control in Pursuit of Her Dream of Becoming a Teacher

Carolina's passion for education and her remarkable journey as a single parent returning to school exemplify resilience and determination. Her story will undoubtedly inspire countless educators and students, profoundly impacting their lives.

From a young age, Carolina's interest in education was evident. She fondly remembers playing school with her sisters, always assuming the role of the "smartest" one. However, reflecting on those childhood days, she regrets inadvertently fostering a dependency among her siblings. Nonetheless, her fascination with teaching persisted.

The first opportunity that allowed Carolina to explore her passion further came when she worked as a lead teacher at a preschool. The experience was fulfilling and motivated her to expand her education and pursue a career in a K-6 classroom setting. This decision marked a significant turning point in Carolina's journey.

Throughout her school years, Carolina encountered several teachers and mentors who played a pivotal role in connecting with her. Their unwavering belief in her unlimited potential left a lasting impression. One advisor, Kim Tomlinson, stood out as someone who believed in Carolina's journey from the beginning. Her words of encouragement, promising to cheer Carolina on as she crossed the stage to receive her bachelor's degree, have remained etched in Carolina's heart. Kim Tomlinson significantly impacted Carolina's life. Not only was she Carolina's advisor, guiding her through enrolling in classes, but she also served as an exceptional mentor dedicated to the noble pursuit of serving others.

Carolina firmly believes that educators have the power to make a difference in someone's life, no matter the level of education they are involved in. She believes that educators can positively impact students' lives, regardless of where they are in their educational journey. This conviction stems from her own experience and Mrs. Tomlinson's profound influence on her. Just as Mrs. Tomlinson made a lasting impact on Carolina's life, Carolina recognizes that educators have the potential to positively shape and inspire students at any stage of their educational journey.

Carolina's view of herself was a mix of confidence and struggle as a student. English was not her first language, and writing posed significant challenges as an English Language Learner (ELL) student. Growing up in a household where her parents had different educational backgrounds, she lacked the support necessary to excel academically—even into adulthood, grammar and vocabulary remain persistent hurdles for Carolina.

Carolina's journey took on an additional layer of complexity as a single parent to three children—Naomi, Chance, and Chase. They became her driving force, her "why." Coming from a background of poverty, Carolina's parents had instilled in her the belief that working after high school was the only path forward. The lack of information and resources due to language barriers further perpetuated this notion. However, Carolina realized that she had the opportunity to break this cycle and provide her children with a different future—one that embraced education as a path to limitless opportunities.

Carolina's realization of her passions was fueled by attributes such as persistence, commitment, and motivation. These qualities enabled her to overcome challenges and setbacks, driven by her unwavering dedication to her children and her desire to succeed. Precise thinking and effective communication played a crucial role in building trust and credibility, allowing Carolina to make meaningful connections and positively impact others. Cultivating self-control helped her navigate distractions and stay focused on her goals, setting high expectations for herself. Empathy, born out of her own experiences, became a powerful tool for understanding and supporting others. Carolina's curiosity and collaborative mindset drove her pursuit of a teaching career, ensuring all students could tap into their unlimited potential. Thinking flexibly and embracing innovation prepared her to tackle challenges in her future classroom. Optimism became her guiding force, empowering her to persevere and maintain a positive mindset throughout her journey.

Carolina's story of resilience and determination has the power to inspire educators, parents, and students alike. By sharing her journey, she not only shapes the lives of her future students but also educates the Hispanic community on the abundant resources available. Every student deserves a gifted education, and Carolina's narrative serves as a beacon of hope, driving positive change and opening doors to a new world of opportunities.[140]

Marguarite, Andrew, Calvin, and Carolina faced challenges, relied on assistance, and persevered through setbacks. Yet, their unwavering passion enabled them to discover their strengths, ultimately helping them nurture each of their gifts. It is heartening to recognize that these attributes can be cultivated and mastered by any student. We all should be able to share our unique gifts with the world, and these stories serve as a reminder of the limitless possibilities within each of us.

140. Aguiar, Carolina, "A Single Mother and Former English Language Learner's Gift to the World," personal communication (interview), July 2023.

In Conclusion

Imagine a comfortable and well-worn path that meanders through a beautiful forest. For years, you have followed this path without question. It has become ingrained in your mind, a familiar and effortless route that guides your every step. The path represents how you think, your beliefs, and the perspectives you have developed over time.

Now, picture a new trail emerging beside the old path. This trail represents a different way of thinking, challenging the established patterns and assumptions that have guided you for so long. It beckons with the promise of discovery, growth, and a broader understanding of the world.

However, stepping onto this new trail requires courage and a willingness to leave behind the comfort of the old path. The new trail is rough and uneven, with unexpected twists and turns. It demands you to question long-held beliefs, confront biases, and be open to unfamiliar ideas.

As you venture onto the new trail, you stumble and face obstacles. The terrain feels unfamiliar, causing doubt and discomfort. The familiar landmarks and signposts that once provided reassurance are absent, leaving you disoriented and unsure of your bearings. It's as if you're reprogramming your mental GPS, recalibrating your thinking patterns.

Changing the way, one thinks, is like forging a new path through uncharted territory. It requires effort, persistence, and a willingness to embrace uncertainty. Just as walking on an untrodden trail can be physically demanding, changing the way you think can be mentally and emotionally challenging.

Along the new trail, you encounter resistance. Your mind naturally clings to what is known, seeking the safety of the familiar. Old habits and deeply ingrained beliefs tug at you, tempting you to retreat to the well-worn path. It takes conscious effort to push through these barriers, to keep going despite the discomfort.

But as you persevere, you notice the beauty and richness of the unexplored landscape. New perspectives emerge, expanding your understanding and opening doors to fresh insights. The more you traverse this new trail, the easier it becomes. Your mind adapts, forming new connections and becoming more flexible in its thinking.

Ultimately, changing the way you think is a transformative journey. It requires stepping out of your comfort zone, embracing the unknown, and challenging the status quo. Like forging a new path through the wilderness, it may be difficult and fraught with obstacles, but the rewards of growth, expanded horizons, and a broader understanding of the world make the journey worthwhile.

Building upon the previous analogy of changing the way one thinks, let's extend it to the concept of redefining gifted education from a traditional model that serves only a select few to one that recognizes the unlimited potential in all students. The reason why I wrote this book was primarily for this purpose.

Imagine that the well-worn path represents the traditional approach to gifted education, where a limited number of students are identified as gifted based on specific criteria and provided with specialized programs and resources. This path has been followed for years, shaping the educational landscape and perpetuating the notion that only a select few possess exceptional abilities.

Now, a new trail emerges alongside the old path, representing a shift in thinking toward a more inclusive approach to gifted education. This new trail recognizes that giftedness exists in various forms and can be found in students from all backgrounds and abilities. It challenges the notion of a fixed and predetermined set of gifted individuals and promotes the belief that every student has unique strengths and talents waiting to be nurtured.

Embarking on this new trail requires a fundamental shift in mindset. It calls for a departure from the idea that giftedness is rare and static and embraces the belief that every student deserves opportunities to explore and develop their unlimited potential. Just as stepping onto the new trail demands a willingness to challenge existing beliefs, reimagining gifted education requires questioning long-held assumptions about intelligence and potential.

As educators venture onto this new trail, they face resistance and skepticism. The deeply ingrained notion that giftedness is a limited resource may create doubt and hesitation. It takes courage to challenge the status quo, advocate for fairness, and strive for an education system that recognizes and cultivates the gifts of all students.

Navigating this new trail involves overcoming obstacles and dismantling barriers to create an inclusive learning environment. It requires educators to identify and tap into students' diverse talents, providing them opportunities for enrichment, challenge, and growth. The trail may be rocky at times, as it involves redesigning the curriculum, implementing flexible instructional strategies, and fostering a culture that values and celebrates every student's unique ability.

As the journey progresses, the benefits of this new approach become apparent. The educational landscape becomes more vibrant and diverse, reflecting all students' multifaceted talents and perspectives. The concept of giftedness expands beyond traditional measures, encompassing creativity, leadership, problem-solving, and other valuable skills. By providing all students with a gifted education, society reaps the rewards of an empowered and capable workforce that is better equipped to tackle future challenges.

Changing our thinking from traditional gifted education for only a few to recognizing and nurturing the gifts of all students is like venturing onto a new trail. It demands a shift in mindset, challenging existing beliefs, and embracing the unlimited potential in every individual. By paving the way, we establish an educational environment that nurtures inclusivity, embraces diversity, and enables every student to recognize the vast array of opportunities available to them throughout their lives. This is beautifully summarized by my close friend and colleague Mike Mattos, who often speaks of a "life filled with endless possibilities."

The question is simple: What would you want for your own child?

Epilogue

"Our deepest fear is not that we are inadequate. Our deepest fear is that we are powerful beyond measure. It is our light, not our darkness that most frightens us. We ask ourselves, Who am I to be brilliant, gorgeous, talented, fabulous? Who are you not to be?... Your playing small does not serve the world. There is nothing enlightened about shrinking so that other people won't feel insecure around you. We are all meant to shine, as children do.... It's not just in some of us; it's in everyone. And as we let our own light shine, we unconsciously give other people permission to do the same. As we are liberated from our own fear, our presence automatically liberates others."

—MARIANNE WILLIAMSON[141]

"Can we describe the school we would want our kid to attend? Can we dream of that school?" These profound questions posed by Bob Eaker continue to echo in my mind as I reflect upon the transformative journey we have undertaken in this book. It is not simply a matter of knowledge or common sense; it is a matter of will. Are we prepared to create schools and classrooms that uplift and empower every child? We have reserved such environments for only a privileged few for far too long.

The information that has unfolded within these pages serves as a reminder of the profound impact education can have on individuals and the generations to come. This photograph captures a moment with

---

141. Williamson, Marianne, *A Return to Love: Reflections on the Principles of A Course in Miracles*, HarperCollins, 1992.

my mother, father, older brother, sister, and me in 1966. I was barely one year old at the time. Behind that image lies a lineage of resilience, determination, and sacrifice stretching back to the 1940s.

During those challenging times, my grandparents, sharecroppers with limited education, were trapped in a cycle of poverty. Yet, when my father expressed his desire to attend college during his senior year of high school, they wholeheartedly supported his dreams. However, if my father pursued higher education, an obstacle stood in their path—the landowner threatened to evict them from their home and the land they worked on.

Undeterred by this injustice, my father chose to forge ahead, leaving behind a family on the verge of displacement. When my dad came home after a break from college, his parents were gone. The landowner had made good on his promise. In spite of this hardship, my father completed his college education, becoming a reading teacher and a principal. His journey exemplified the transformative power of education, a force that would shape my own experiences.

I was privileged to have parents who provided abundant opportunities for my siblings and me throughout my upbringing. Nevertheless, I encountered challenges when it came to learning how to read. However, the support and resources available to me, coupled with the unwavering belief in my unlimited potential instilled by my parents, enabled me to overcome those hurdles. I recognize that not all children are as fortunate to have the same level of support at home in their areas of need. This is where my passion comes from.

The sacrifices of my grandparents and my parents' dedication altered my life's trajectory and influenced the lives of my children, Alison and Emily. Their commitment to education created a ripple effect that continues to shape and inspire me today.

This personal story, interwoven with the lessons learned throughout this book, has solidified my belief in nurturing each student's unique strengths, passions, and talents. The five shifts we have explored—dismissing fixed intelligence fallacies, shedding harmful labels, embracing collective teacher efficacy and collective responsibility, providing students and teachers with their superpowers, and addressing resistance and finding inspiration in the success of others—serve as guiding principles to transform gifted education from a privilege for a few into a universal reality.

If you are hesitant to make these shifts, I implore you to consider the choices before you. Will you uphold the status quo, perpetuating a system that serves only a select few? Or will you join me in aligning your mission with action, ushering in an era in which we believe every student deserves a gifted education?

Let us not be intimidated by the challenges that lie ahead. Instead, let us draw inspiration from the words of Nelson Mandela, who believed, "It's not beyond our power to create a world where every child has access to a quality education"[142]—an education that brings freedom, unleashes unlimited potential, and opens doors to unforeseen opportunities.

---

142. Nelson Mandela Institute for Education and Rural Development, https://www.mandelainstitute.org.za/.

I am driven by the gift of a life my grandparents could have only dreamed of. My parents showed me their love, time, experience, expertise, and unwavering belief in my unlimited learning capacity. Now, it is my responsibility to share that gift with the world.

We can change the narrative around gifted education through our collective efforts. We can create classrooms where every student's unique strengths, passions, and talents are cultivated and celebrated. By embracing these five shifts, we can make gifted education the foundation of every classroom.

As I conclude this book, I carry a profound sense of purpose and an unwavering dedication to influencing the world to ensure that every child's gifts are cherished and nurtured. Together, let us embark on this transformative journey, knowing that through education, we have the power to shape a brighter and more equitable future for all.

In addition, I must express my heartfelt gratitude to those individuals who played pivotal roles in shaping my educational journey. Ms. Brenda Cox and the late Ann Stephenson, my high school physics and history teachers, made me feel "smart" every day I walked into their classrooms. Their unwavering support, belief in my abilities, and dedication to me as an individual gave me confidence as a student for the first time.

I am also indebted to my high school basketball coach, William Butch Waller, who honed my skills on the court and instilled in me the values of discipline, teamwork, and perseverance. Coach Waller saw something in me, allowed me to shine, and helped me secure a Division I basketball scholarship to The George Washington University. This opportunity opened a new world, granting me access to higher education and experiences I could have only dreamed of.

To all the family, friends, educators, colleagues, and mentors, thank you for being the catalysts of change in my life. Your belief in my unlimited potential, guidance, and unwavering support are forever etched in my heart. Your influence resonates in my work and serves as a constant reminder of the profound impact educators can have on the lives of their students.

As we conclude this book, let's not lose sight of the countless individuals who've played a pivotal role in shaping our own journeys, guiding us, and affording us opportunities to shine. Together, through our united efforts, we can forge educational environments where every student is nurtured, celebrated, and empowered to share their gifts with the world.

Acknowledgments

In the face of a professional challenge, I decided to change directions in 2021. The decision was daunting, akin to starting anew. While much of my educational consulting had centered around a specific domain, I realized that my identity as an educator remained unknown to many beyond that realm. Yet, fueled by a dream and a passion for sharing what I had lived as a school principal with my coprincipal partners, Diane Kerr and Sherry Shin, I recognized the imperative to shape my thoughts through words.

I spent a few years drifting without genuinely dedicating myself to writing this book. Then, a pivotal moment arrived. An epiphany washed over me, revealing that my wife, Kathleen, and accomplished daughters, Alison and Emily, guided me in more profound ways than words. Their actions reminded me that I needed to find my spark again and shine my light on this extremely important issue: helping educators nurture each student's unique strengths, passions, and talents.

In the spring of 2023, drawing inspiration from my daughter Alison's TEDx event and discussions with my dear friend Steve Frick, who shared that he was transitioning from a full-time pediatric orthopedic surgeon to taking on a more prominent role leading a national medical organization, I decided to write this book. I am grateful for the unwavering support of Ken Williams, author of *Ruthless Equity*. Ken propelled me forward as he provided guidance and introduced me to essential contacts, expediting my writing process.

Foremost among those who deserve my gratitude is Martha Bullen, my book coach and guiding light. Her expert navigation through the complexities of publishing has been invaluable. Christy Day, the creative force behind the book's cover and interior design, and David Aretha, my editor, joined me on this transformative journey. Together, within six months, we breathed life into this book.

A circle of people for whom I am deeply thankful kept me on course. This esteemed group includes colleagues and friends who became champions of my passion project in various ways. I extend my gratitude to Tracey Hulen, Robyn Dawson, Sherri Shin, Charletta Ayers, Jack Baldermann, Paula Rogers, Regina Owens, Morgan Huynh, Jaivon Smallwood, Paula Maeker, Aaron Hanson, Richard Rockenbach, Monica Buckhorn, Sandra Miracle, Sarah Trevino, Greg Taylor, Darryl Webster, Michael O'Reilly, Julie Schmidt, Doug Gee, Zandra Galvin, Michael Nagler, Sandy Mallon, John Mallon, Willie Benton, Mark Ausbrooks, Christie Yarn, Ashley Friend, Nicole Dimich, Johanna Saa, Craig Helms, Eric Burrell, Kimberley Mathews, Liz Scheurer, Jessica Bagnall, Hannah Aldridge-Collins, Marguarite Gooden, Calvin Barnes, Carolina Aguiar, Tom Hierck, Alex Kajitani, Debbie McDonald, Andrew Mallon, Don Parker, Katie Koeppel, Katie White, Tom Many, Louise Robertson, Lindsay Ek, Nicole Vide, Chris Jerry, Leslie Leisey, Bob Eaker, Jessica and John Hannigan, Beth English, Jenn Deinhart, Tina Boogren, Tim Kanold, Jack Dale, Laura Waggoner, Jeff Craig, Jeannie Spiller, Lynn Brosner, Charles Brooks, Brian Levy, and Tom Schimmer.

Diane Kerr, Jacquie Heller, Geri Parscale, and Robyn Dawson, thank you for being such faithful accountability partners. This book would be far from what it is had I not benefitted from your honesty and feedback.

Anthony Muhammad, Mike Mattos, Luis Cruz, Mike Brown, Ken Barer, Bill Ferriter, and Gavin Grift, no matter what, answered my texts, calls, and pleas for assistance over the past few years. You are the best! While I may have missed acknowledging a few others who helped me on this journey, they know they are part of this tribute.

I must acknowledge my late grandparents, Lulu and Romie Butler, Charles and Sarah Ayers, who were born in the late 1800s and early 1900s. Their sacrifices and dreams are being realized through their grandson. To my parents, Doris and the late Paul Butler, your unwavering support, guidance, and belief in my unlimited potential have made this achievement possible. I appreciate my brother Paul and sister Monica, who have made my path a bit easier by being my older siblings who paved the way first.

I admire educational luminaries such as Yvette Jackson, Gholdy Muhammad, Zaretta Hammond, Carol Dweck, Eric Jensen, Baruti Kafele, Joseph Renzulli, and Carol Tomlinson. Their profound ideas have left an indelible mark on my work, even though our paths have not crossed.

As I go forward, I hope my three education heroes—Richard DuFour, Rebecca DuFour, and Carolyn Miller—look down with smiles, aware of their influence within these pages.

Although their names may not grace these acknowledgments, the stories in this book are woven with countless individuals who have guided and inspired me. These fictionalized accounts pay homage to people who have impacted my educational journey. These remarkable people had a massive influence on my journey.

"As I go, I am wearing you."
—AFRICAN PROVERB

About the Author

 Brian Butler is an educational consultant, speaker, author, and award-winning former principal who is passionate about nurturing collaborative school cultures that unlock the unlimited potential in every student. Brian has advised thousands of schools across the United States, Australia, and Canada. His expertise lies in coaching teacher teams, guiding school leadership, and fostering principal-administrator team collaborations.

Drawing on the latest research and evidence-based practices, Brian empowers educators to believe in their role as catalysts for student empowerment. He focuses on harnessing the collective knowledge, skills, and experiences within school communities. Brian's ultimate goal is to help schools and districts realize that the key to success is often found within their walls, which inspired him to name his company The Answer's In The Room.

Brian is the author of *Every Student Deserves a Gifted Education: 5 Shifts to Nurturing Each Student's Unique Strengths, Passions, and Talents*. He is coauthor of *What About Us? The PLC at Work Process for Grades PreK-2 Teams* and a contributing author of *It's About Time: Planning Interventions and Extensions in Elementary Schools*.

Brian has enjoyed diverse career experiences, including playing professional basketball in the European League. He holds a bachelor's degree in speech communications from The George Washington University, a teacher's certification in physical education, and a master's degree in school counseling from George Mason University. With an administrative endorsement from the University of Virginia, Brian is known for his ability to drive positive change.

Beyond his professional achievements, Brian and his wife Kathleen are proud parents to two adult daughters, Alison and Emily. Brian and Kathleen live in northern Virginia. To learn more or contact Brian, visit www.brianbutler.info.

Made in the USA
Middletown, DE
09 November 2023

42150563R00156